DEAD *and* ALIVE

Thanks to Jen Williams for transcribing Jim's lectures on obedience and to Lisa Just for putting them together as a book.

Published by Community Christian Ministries
P.O. Box 9754, Moscow, Idaho 83843
208.883.0997 | www.ccmbooks.org

Jim Wilson, *Dead and Alive: Obedience and the New Man*
Copyright © 2016 by James I. Wilson

Excerpts from *The Father and His Family* used in Appendix A © 1964, Gospel Publishing Society. Used by permission.

Cover photos: "Cracked earth" (https://www.flickr.com/photos/happy_gecko/2294941045), by Flickr user Happy Gecko; untitled (https://www.flickr.com/photos/eamathe/10254391486/) by Flickr user Emily Matthews. Both licensed under CC BY 2.0 (https://creativecommons.org/licenses/by/2.0/). Both cropped from original.

Author photo by Mark LaMoreaux, lamoreauxphoto.com.

Unless otherwise stated, all Scripture quotations are from the the Holy Bible, New International Version®, niv® Copyright © 1973, 1978, 1984, 2011 by Biblica, Inc.® Used by permission. All rights reserved worldwide.

Scripture quotations marked esv are from The Holy Bible, English Standard Version Copyright © 2001 by Crossway Bibles, a publishing ministry of Good News Publishers.

Scripture quotations marked kjv are from the King James Version.

Scripture quotations marked nkjv are from the New King James Version®. Copyright © 1982 by Thomas Nelson. Used by permission. All rights reserved.

Scripture quotations marked phillips are from the New Testament in Modern English by J.B Phillips copyright © 1960, 1972 J. B. Phillips. Administered by The Archbishops' Council of the Church of England. Used by permission.

Scripture quotations marked rsv are from the Revised Standard Version of the Bible, copyright © 1946, 1952, and 1971 the Division of Christian Education of the National Council of the Churches of Christ in the United States of America. Used by permission. All rights reserved.

Any italics in Scripture quotations have been added by the author for emphasis.

Cover and interior design by Valerie Anne Bost
Printed in the United States of America.

16 17 18 19 20 21 22 23   9 8 7 6 5 4 3 2 1

DEAD *and* ALIVE

obedience and the new man

JIM WILSON
edited by Lisa Just

COMMUNITY
CHRISTIAN
MINISTRIES
MOSCOW, IDAHO
www.ccmbooks.org

CONTENTS

APPENDICES

To Matt Meyer, who learned it and lived it.

INTRODUCTION

This book was written primarily to help new Christians anticipate an obedient, victorious life in Christ. It was also written to encourage defeated Christians who think defeat is normal.

For hundreds of years, the church has struggled with how to explain and overcome disobedience. We know that the cross takes care of our past sins and our life after death, but we don't know what to do with the time in between salvation and death.

When born-again Christians have sin problems, they need to come up with a way to get victory over them. Here are a few of the solutions the church has proposed over the centuries as ways for Christians to live obedient and victorious lives:

- Roman Catholic Church: vows, monasticism, confession, and penance
- Wesleyan/Holiness Theology: a second work of grace subsequent to the new birth, called "sanctification"
- Dispensational churches: a second event called "making Jesus Lord of your life"
- Pentecostal churches: the baptism of the Holy Spirit, which gives you the power to live the Christian life
- Southern Baptist Church: rededicating your life
- Keswick Convention: receiving the Holy Spirit
- Evangelical churches: reckoning yourself dead to sin, even though you are still struggling against the old nature

There are three problems with these solutions:

1. They are not biblical.
2. They are man-centered rather than Christ-centered.
3. They do not work.

The Bible mentions two great works of Jesus Christ: His death and resurrection and His Second Coming. When you believe in His death and resurrection, you receive the Holy Spirit, which is the down-payment, the guarantee of the resurrection of your body at the Second Coming:

> And you also were included in Christ when you heard the word of truth, the gospel of your salvation. Having believed, you were marked in him with a seal, the promised *Holy Spirit*, who is *a deposit* guaranteeing *our inheritance* until the redemption

> of those who are God's possession—to the praise of his glory. (Eph. 1:13–14)

> It is because of him that you are in Christ Jesus, who has become for us wisdom from God—that is, our righteousness, holiness and redemption. (1 Cor. 1:30)

By His death and resurrection, Jesus Christ provided our justification, our sanctification, and the redemption of our bodies. He has provided it *all*.

> And those he predestined, he also called; those he called, he also *justified*; those he justified, he also *glorified*. (Rom. 8:30)

> Now if we *died with Christ*, we believe that *we will also live with him*. (Rom. 6:8)

> *For you died*, and your life is now hidden with Christ in God. (Col. 3:3)

This is the key. Christ's death and resurrection go together. Because of them, we who have trusted in Jesus have received forgiveness of sins and a place among those who are sanctified by faith in Him. Is there something more than "forgiveness" and "a place among the sanctified"? There is. This book is about that "something more," which is the third result of the death and resurrection of Jesus Christ and our faith in Him. That result is obedience.

We died with Christ. Our sinful nature was crucified with Him. This is in the past tense. It has happened already.

We have been raised with Christ. We live in Him. We live by the Spirit. We are alive in Christ. This is *already* true.

I have included an appendix quoting from E.W. Kenyon's book, *The Father and His Family*. My first hunger for Christ came under his preaching in 1936 when I was 8 years old.

In the Lord Jesus Christ,
JIM WILSON, 2016

BACKGROUND
to OBEDIENCE

CHAPTER I

THE BASIS FOR OBEDIENCE

For he chose us in him before the creation of the world
to be holy and blameless in his sight. (Eph. 1:4)

There are two main reasons for our obedience to God. They both have to do with Him.

WHO HE IS

In the past God spoke to our forefathers through the prophets at many times and in various ways, but in these last days he has spoken to us by his Son, whom he appointed heir of all things, and through whom he made the universe. (Heb. 1:1–2)

> He is the image of the invisible God, the firstborn over all creation. (Col. 1:15)

> In the beginning was the Word, and the Word was with God, and the Word was God. (John 1:1)

WHAT HE HAS DONE

He created us.

> For by him all things were created: things in heaven and on earth, visible and invisible, whether thrones or powers or rulers or authorities; all things were created by him and for him. (Col. 1:16)

> Through him all things were made; without him nothing was made that has been made. (John 1:3)

> By the word of the Lord were the heavens made, their starry host by the breath of his mouth. He gathers the waters of the sea into jars; he puts the deep into storehouses. Let all the earth fear the Lord; let all the people of the world revere him. For he spoke, and it came to be; he commanded, and it stood firm. (Psalm 33:6–9)

> You are worthy, our Lord and God, to receive glory and honor and power, for you created all things, and by your will they were created and have their being. (Rev. 4:11)

He redeemed us.

> For God was pleased to have all his fullness dwell in him, and through him to reconcile to himself all

> things, whether things on earth or things in heaven, by making peace through his blood, shed on the cross. (Col. 1:19–20)

> Yet to all who received him, to those who believed in his name, he gave the right to become children of God. (John 1:12)

> This righteousness from God comes through faith in Jesus Christ to all who believe. There is no difference, for all have sinned and fall short of the glory of God, and are justified freely by his grace through the redemption that came by Christ Jesus. God presented him as a sacrifice of atonement, through faith in his blood. He did this to demonstrate his justice, because in his forbearance he had left the sins committed beforehand unpunished. (Rom. 3:22–25)

In the following chapters, I will discuss many other reasons for obedience that are subordinate to these. Most of them center on our redemption in Christ.

As Christians, we know the wonder, the reality, and the truth of the forgiveness of sins. The Bible tells us about this forgiveness in many places. Here are a few of them:

> For I will forgive their wickedness and will remember their sins no more. (Heb. 8:12)

> I will rescue you from your own people and from the Gentiles. I am sending you to them to open their eyes and turn them from darkness to light, and from the power of Satan to God, so that they may receive forgiveness of sins and a place among those who are sanctified by faith in me. (Acts 26:17–18)

> He told them, "This is what is written: The Christ will
> suffer and rise from the dead on the third day, and
> repentance and forgiveness of sins will be preached
> in his name to all nations, beginning at Jerusalem."
> (Luke 24:46–47)

After we are forgiven, God both expects and requires us
to be obedient. This obedience is different from the obedience we had (or attempted to have) before receiving Christ.
Our pre-Christian obedience was by effort and willpower.
It was motivated by the threat of unpleasant consequences.
It might also have been motivated by love for the one who
gave the command, but even that kind of obedience can be
half-hearted, foot-dragging, and reluctant. It is hard for us
to think of obedience as anything different from this. But
we must. Christian obedience is meant to be *glad, willing,
and normal.*

Obedience is very much like forgiveness. It was paid for
at the cross and is ours through grace. It is called *sanctification.* Here are a few verses describing the obedience that
follows our receiving Christ:

> For it is by grace you have been saved, through
> faith—and this not from yourselves, it is the gift of
> God—not by works, so that no one can boast. For we
> are God's workmanship, created in Christ Jesus to do
> good works, which God prepared in advance for us
> to do. (Eph. 2:8–10)

> But when the kindness and love of God our Savior ap-
> peared, he saved us, not because of righteous things

we had done, but because of his mercy. He saved us through the washing of rebirth and renewal by the Holy Spirit, whom he poured out on us generously through Jesus Christ our Savior, so that, having been justified by his grace, we might become heirs having the hope of eternal life. This is a trustworthy saying. And I want you to stress these things, so that those who have trusted in God may be careful to devote themselves to doing what is good. These things are excellent and profitable for everyone. (Titus 3:4–8)

My dear children, I write this to you so that you will not sin. But if anybody does sin, we have one who speaks to the Father in our defense—Jesus Christ, the Righteous One. (1 John 2:1)

His divine power has given us everything we need for life and godliness through our knowledge of him who called us by his own glory and goodness. (2 Pet. 1:3)

May the following thoughts lead you into a gracious, obedient life.

CHAPTER 2

THE NATURAL MAN: DEAD IN SIN

As for you, you were dead in your transgressions and sins, in which you used to live when you followed the ways of this world and of the ruler of the kingdom of the air, the spirit who is now at work in those who are disobedient. (Eph. 2:1–2)

Man's nature is tied to two great realities: the nature of God and the nature of the Tree of the Knowledge of Good and Evil.

> Then God said, "Let Us make man in Our image, according to Our likeness; let them have dominion over the fish of the sea, over the birds of the air, and over the cattle, over all the earth and over every creeping thing

> that creeps on the earth." So God created man in His
> own image; in the image of God He created him; male
> and female He created them. Then God blessed them,
> and God said to them, "Be fruitful and multiply; fill the
> earth and subdue it; have dominion over the fish of the
> sea, over the birds of the air, and over every living thing
> that moves on the earth." (Gen. 1:26–28 NKJV)

> And out of the ground the LORD God made every tree
> grow that is pleasant to the sight and good for food. The
> tree of life was also in the midst of the garden, and the
> tree of the knowledge of good and evil. (Gen. 2:9 NKJV)

> Then the LORD God took the man and put him in the
> garden of Eden to tend and keep it. (Gen. 2:15 NKJV)

Man started out with the likeness of God. In Genesis 1:26, God expresses His purpose to make man in "our image, after our likeness; and let them have dominion." In verses 27 and 28, He works according to this plan. He creates, commands reproduction, gives man dominion over the rest of creation, blesses him, and is satisfied with His work.

Some of man's likeness to God did not come from being created in His image:

> And the LORD God said, *"The man has now become
> like one of us,* knowing good and evil. He must not
> be allowed to reach out his hand and take also from
> the tree of life and eat, and live forever." (Gen. 3:22)

Because man disobeyed God by eating of the tree of the knowledge of good and evil, he *became like God* in that he knew good and evil.

When man sinned, his dominion was not taken away, nor was his responsibility to be fruitful and multiply. The blessing he received at creation was not taken away, either. The serpent was cursed, and the ground was cursed, but the man and the woman were not.

Through the tree of life, man had the possibility of living forever. Instead, he chose the tree of death and died. This death was the result of sin. Romans 5:12 says that sin came into the world through that one man and death through sin.

Sin came into the world through one man. Death spread to all men because all men sin. And all men sin because the first man sinned.

> For if many died through one man's trespass... (Rom. 5:15 ESV)

> For if, because of one man's trespass, death reigned through that one man.... (Rom. 5:17 ESV)

> Therefore, as one trespass led to condemnation for all men... (Rom. 5:18 ESV)

> For as by the one man's disobedience the many were made sinners... (Rom. 5:19 ESV)

Man acquired three things because of the Fall:

1. Tendency to sin
2. Knowledge of the difference between good and evil, right and wrong
3. Mortality

Mankind has tried to solve the problem of sin since the beginning. He thinks that if he learns the difference between right and wrong and wants to do right, he can do it. But the theory does not hold water. Every individual on the planet could find hundreds of instances in his own life where he knew what was right and did not do it. Man knows the difference between good and evil and wants to be good, but *does evil anyway.* Yet he clings to theories that say he can be good, because he would rather earn his way to heaven than surrender his life to Christ.

The man without Christ cannot keep from doing evil even if he tries very hard. Although he has dominion over the plants and animals, he has lost dominion over himself. That power was handed over to Satan.

> And you He made alive, when you were dead through the trespasses and sins in which you once walked, following the course of this world, following the prince of the power of the air, the spirit that is now at work in the sons of disobedience. Among these we all once lived in the passions of our flesh, following the desires of body and mind, and so we were by nature children of wrath, like the rest of mankind. (Eph. 2:1–3 RSV)

> And they may escape from the snare of the devil, after *being captured by him to do his will.* (2 Tim. 2:26 RSV)

The natural man (the unsaved, unregenerate man) is under interior control by Satan. He is an integral part of the world system controlled by the devil and has a very influential role in running it.[1] In fact, he is essential to it. Satan is the mind of the system, but the natural man is its heart and limbs.

> Now is the judgment of the world, now shall *the ruler of this world* be cast out. (John 12:31 RSV)

> I will no longer talk much with you, for *the ruler of this world* is coming. He has no power over Me. (John 14:30 RSV)

> And when he comes, he will convince the world concerning sin and righteousness and judgment: concerning sin, because they do not believe in me... concerning judgment, because the ruler of this world is judged. (John 16:8–9, 11 RSV)

Because he is under Satan's control, the natural man has prostituted the responsibility of dominion by using nature for his own immediate pleasures. He has also perverted the command to be fruitful with his sins of pornography, prostitution, polygamy, free love, and abortion. This has resulted in the degeneracy of complete societies (e.g., Sodom, Corinth, and Rome). All men may not commit all of these sins, but each person is influenced by them and influences others. Societal decay would progress much faster if it were not for the retarding influences of the Christian man and his laws.

When the natural man worships, he creates religions that involve observing a moral code. When he builds cities, he forms a criminal code on this same sense of right

1 See *Love Not the World* by Watchman Nee for a more complete statement.

and wrong. He incorporates his knowledge of good and evil into his religion and his laws for several reasons:

1. Knowing good and evil is part of his nature, so it is natural for him to include them.
2. It is also natural for him to violate his sense of right, so having morality in his religion provides extra motivation to do what he knows he ought to do.
3. Having the moral law in the criminal code is an even greater and more immediate motivation to keep from doing wrong.

But we know that the law is good if one uses it lawfully, knowing this: that the law is not made for a righteous person, but for the lawless and insubordinate, for the ungodly and for sinners, for the unholy and profane, for murderers of fathers and murderers of mothers, for manslayers, for fornicators, for sodomites, for kidnappers, for liars, for perjurers, and if there is any other thing that is contrary to sound doctrine, according to the glorious gospel of the blessed God which was committed to my trust. (1 Tim. 1:8–11 NKJV)

the SPIRITUAL MAN

CHAPTER 3

THE SPIRITUAL MAN: DEAD TO SIN, ALIVE IN CHRIST

*By no means! We are those who have died to sin;
how can we live in it any longer? (Rom. 6:2)*

Unlike the natural man, the Christian man has the power to do the good he wills—because of Christ.

> His divine power has given us *everything we need for life and godliness* through our knowledge of him who called us by his own glory and goodness. Through these he has given us his very great and precious promises, so that through them you may participate in the divine nature and escape the corruption in the world caused by evil desires. (2 Pet. 1:3–4)

At the Fall, we became like God by knowing good and evil, but unlike Him by becoming subject to death and an inherent tendency to rebel against Him. This tendency is also known as being under the law of sin.

When a man turns to God through Jesus Christ, he is freed from the law of sin. He lives forever with an inheritance that is imperishable, undefiled, and unfading, and he is made a partaker of the divine nature. He loses the law of sin at conversion. He *loses* his old nature. The Christian is no longer a natural man.

> For to be carnally minded is death, but to be spiritually minded is life and peace. Because the carnal mind is enmity against God; for it is not subject to the law of God, nor indeed can be. So then, those who are in the flesh cannot please God. But you are not in the flesh but in the Spirit, if indeed the Spirit of God dwells in you. Now if anyone does not have the Spirit of Christ, he is not His. (Rom. 8:6–9 NKJV)

Let us look at this passage in reverse order. If anyone does not have the Spirit of Christ, he does not belong to Christ. However, if the Spirit of God dwells in you, then you are in the Spirit; and consequently, you are not in the flesh. The word "you" applies to every Christian. This is true regardless of how you feel. Truth comes from God by revelation. It does not come from our feelings.

Look at Romans 6, 1 Corinthians 6 and 10, 2 Corinthians 5, Ephesians 4, and Galatians 5. The teaching in these texts is unequivocal. In discussing them, I will assume without running through a proof here that the terms "old self," "old nature," and "the flesh" are basically synonymous.

> For we know that our *old self was crucified with him* so that the body of sin might be done away with, that we should no longer be slaves to sin. (Rom. 6:6)

> Now if *we died with Christ*, we believe that we will also live with him. For we know that since Christ was raised from the dead, he cannot die again; death no longer has mastery over him. The death he died, he died to sin once for all; but the life he lives, he lives to God. In the same way, *count yourselves dead to sin* but alive to God in Christ Jesus. (Rom. 6:8–11)

The slaveholder within us is dead, that henceforth we should not serve him. Our old self was crucified with Him, so *act* like it was. Count yourselves dead to sin. How? You *are* dead to sin. *Simply choose to believe it.*

"What shall we say, then? Shall we go on sinning so that grace may increase? By no means! We *died* to sin; how can we live in it any longer?" (Rom. 6:1–2). Scripture makes a distinction between being dead *to* something and being dead *in* it. If I am dead *in* sin, that means I am stuck in it, lost in it, so to speak. If I am dead *to* sin, I have been separated from it.

"Or don't you know that all of us who were baptized into Christ Jesus were baptized into his death?" (Rom. 6:3). Don't you know that?

"We were therefore buried with him through baptism into death in order that, just as Christ was raised from the dead through the glory of the Father, we too may live *a new life*" (Rom. 6:4). When we received Christ, we entered into His death, His burial, and His resurrection so that we might live a new life.

"If we have been united with him like this in his death, we will certainly also be united with him in his resurrection" (Rom. 6:5). If we *have been* (past event), we *will certainly be* (future event).

Death is instantaneous and occurs only once. Life occurs after death, and Christ lives unto God. Christ died to sin once, though He had no sin of His own. It was our sin He died to. Isaiah 53 and 2 Corinthians 5 tell us:

> Surely He has borne our griefs and carried our sorrows; yet we esteemed Him stricken, smitten by God, and afflicted. But He was wounded *for our transgressions*, He was bruised *for our iniquities*; upon Him was the chastisement that made us whole, and with His stripes we are healed. All we like sheep have gone astray; we have turned every one to his own way; and *the* LORD *has laid on Him the iniquity of us all.* (Isa. 53:4–6 RSV)

> For our sake he made Him to be sin who knew no sin, so that in Him we might become the righteousness of God. (2 Cor. 5:21 RSV)

Christ died to sin. We are *dead* to sin. He arose! We are alive unto God through Jesus Christ our Lord. The old man is dead. This is a fact. The Bible does not tell us to imagine that our old man is dead. We are not playing make-believe in a cowboys-and-Indians fashion, nor was Jesus when He died unto sin once. But whether we understand this or not, believe it or not, makes no difference to the *facts*. If you are a Christian, your old man is dead.

Why does it matter if we believe the old man is still alive? It matters because by doing that, we create an excuse for sin. We think we can blame our disobedience on the "old man" (who is imaginary now), when in reality we are sinning by choice.

There is a correlation in the New Testament between the superlative requirements which are placed upon us...

> You, therefore, must *be perfect*, as your heavenly Father is perfect. (Matt. 5:48 RSV)

> My dear children, *I write this to you so that you will not sin*. But if anybody does sin, we have one who speaks to the Father in our defense—Jesus Christ, the Righteous One. (1 John 2:1)

> But just as he who called you is holy, so *be holy in all you do*; for it is written: "Be holy, because I am holy." (1 Pet. 1:15–16)

...and the divine nature God has given us:

> *His divine power has given us everything we need for life and godliness* through our knowledge of him who called us by his own glory and goodness. (2 Pet. 1:3)

> And that is what some of you were. But *you were washed, you were sanctified, you were justified* in the name of the Lord Jesus Christ and by the Spirit of our God. (1 Cor. 6:11)

> Therefore, if anyone is in Christ, he is a new creation;
> the old has gone, the new has come! (2 Cor. 5:17)

If these statements are false, then Peter and Paul were telling whoppers about God, and the Bible cannot be trusted. If they are true, then we do not lack anything for living the Christian life in godliness and holiness. Let us thank God and praise Him.

The work of Christ on the cross was not just for our forgiveness of sins and our future inheritance. It was also for the life between our new birth and our going to be with Him. If we only count on the forgiveness God provides us each time we sin, we are living out a truncated view of His grace. Jesus died so that we would not sin in the first place. He gave us a new nature so that we would not sin. He commands us not to sin.

> My dear children, I write this to you *so that you will not sin.* (1 John 2:1a)

> But now you must rid yourselves of all such things as these: anger, rage, malice, slander, and filthy language from your lips. Do not lie to each other, since *you have taken off your old self with its practices and have put on the new self,* which is being renewed in knowledge in the image of its Creator. (Col. 3:8–10)

Why are Christians not to lie to each other? Because of something that happened to us. What happened? We took off our old self with its practices. We also put on the new nature, which is being renewed (made newer and newer all the time) in the knowledge of its Creator. The two natures do not coexist. At your conversion, you took off the old, and you put on the new.

What does this mean for us? "So I tell you this, and insist on it in the Lord, that *you must no longer live as the Gentiles do* in the futility of their thinking. They are darkened in their understanding, separated from the life of God, because of the ignorance that is in them due to the hardening of their hearts. Having lost all sensitivity, they have given themselves over to sensuality so as to indulge in every kind of impurity with a continual lust for more" (Eph. 4:17–19). This is a description of the pagan world. The Gentiles live in sin naturally, because their understanding is darkened, because they are alienated from the life of God. Paul says we must not live that way, and the implication is that if we do, we are living that way *by choice*. When you sin, it is not natural. A Christian *cannot* blame his sin on his old nature. He doesn't have one. "I insist on it in the Lord, that you must no longer live like these people," Paul says.

Why? "You, however, did not come to know Christ that way" (Eph. 4:20). Which way? In a way where you could be a Christian and still live like the devil. Christ did not give us eternal life and forgiveness so that we could keep living in darkness.

When you first heard about Jesus Christ, this licentiousness is not what you learned. "Surely you heard of him [past tense] and were taught in him [past tense] in accordance with the truth that is in Jesus" (Eph. 4:21). You already learned this back when you came to know Christ. "*You were taught*, with regard to your former way of life, *to put off your old self,* which is being corrupted by its deceitful desires" (Eph. 4:22). "Is being corrupted" is present tense, but it is present tense within the framework of the past tense sentence: when you had that old self, it was being corrupted. You were taught to put it off, "to be made new in the attitude of your minds; and to put on the new self, created to be like God in true righteousness and holiness" (Eph. 4:23–24).

Paul does not say you are to put off the old nature *now.* If you are a Christian, it has already been done. Even if you believe that Paul was telling the Ephesians to put off their old nature right then, as Christians, he still did *not* say to place the new man, righteous and holy, *on top of* the corrupt old man. The text does not allow for both the old man and the new man to live together in the same person. You must put off the one before you put on the other.

Of course, next to all of these verses about the new man, there is strong instruction that we should not live as we did when we had the old man. Apparently we can still sin after we are saved, or this instruction would not be necessary.

"No temptation has seized you except what is common to man. And God is faithful; he will not let you be tempted beyond what you can bear. But when you are tempted, he will also provide a way out so that you can stand up under it" (1 Cor. 10:13). Paul tells us specifically that God is faithful and will provide a way out of any temptation. He has made it so that we do not have to sin. However, being a new man does not make us robots where righteousness is programmed in and holiness is by the numbers. No—we are free men. In this way, we are like both pre-fall Adam and Jesus, who is called the last Adam.[2] Both were free men. They were not slaves to sin. However, they were both primary targets for the tempter. Adam was tempted and sinned by choice. He did not need an old nature in order to be tempted or in order to sin. Jesus was tempted in all points as we are, yet without sin. He did not need an old nature in order to be tempted. He never had one. We do not have an old nature, either. If we sin, we sin by choice.

There are several passages often quoted in an attempt to establish the existence of both natures in believers. One of them is Galatians 5:16–17.[3] This passage is easy to quote out of context. "But I say, walk by the Spirit, and do not gratify the desires of the flesh. For the desires of the flesh are against the Spirit, and the desires of the Spirit are against the flesh; for these are opposed to each other, to prevent you from doing what you would" (RSV).

This passage makes it sound like the flesh and the Spirit are coexistent, fighting away in the believer; but if you read the verses around it, it becomes obvious that that is not the case: "But if you are led by the Spirit you are not under the law. Now the works of the flesh are plain: fornication, impurity, licentiousness, idolatry, sorcery, enmity, strife, jealousy, anger, selfishness, dissension, party spirit, envy, drunkenness, carousing, and the like. I warn you, as I warned you before, that those who do such things shall not inherit the kingdom of God. But the fruit of the Spirit

2   1 Corinthians 15
3   The other passage is Romans 7, which will be discussed in the next chapter.

is love, joy, peace, patience, kindness, goodness, faithfulness, gentleness, self-control; against such there is no law" (Gal. 5:18–23 rsv).

Look carefully at Galatians 5:24: "And those who belong to Christ Jesus have crucified the flesh with its passions and desires" (rsv). Just by belonging to Jesus, we have crucified the flesh. And those with the works of the flesh shall not inherit the kingdom of God. There *is* a war between the flesh and the Spirit, but it is not an *interior* war. It is the same war described by Ephesians 6:12: "For our struggle is not against flesh and blood, but against the rulers, against the authorities, against the powers of this dark world and against the spiritual forces of evil in the heavenly realms."

What I have laid out in this chapter is not a complete picture of the Christian. It is an attempt to open your understanding to the teaching of the New Testament on what is available to you in Christ *now*. Statements like, "You, therefore, must be perfect, as your heavenly Father is perfect" (Matt. 5:48 rsv) and, "But just as he who called you is holy, so be holy in all you do" (1 Pet. 1:15) are to be taken seriously. They are not impossible ideals, because God provides us the grace. His standards of holiness are not inconsistent with His provision for holiness.4

The Lord Jesus Christ has prayed for all Christians: "My prayer is not that you take them out of the world but that you protect them from the evil one. *They are not of the world, even as I am not of it.*..My prayer is not for them

4 I recommend reading *Victory in Christ* by Charles Trumbull for more on this subject.

alone. I pray also for those who will believe in me through their message" (John 17:15–16, 20).

Here we are—millions of Christians scattered in the world among hundreds of millions of natural men. We have a primary objective: to be like the Lord Jesus. Our secondary objective is the evangelization of the rest of the world.

> You are the light of the world. (Matt. 5:14)

> Therefore go and make disciples of all nations, baptizing them in the name of the Father and of the Son and of the Holy Spirit, and teaching them to obey everything I have commanded you. And surely I am with you always, to the very end of the age. (Matt. 28:19–20)

We also have a third objective—to influence the world for good and for peace.

> *You are the salt of the earth.* But if the salt loses its saltiness, how can it be made salty again? It is no longer good for anything, except to be thrown out and trampled by men. (Matt. 5:13)

> First of all, then, I urge that supplications, prayers, intercessions, and thanksgivings be made for all men, for kings and all who are in high positions, that we may *lead a quiet and peaceable life, godly and respectful in every way.* (1 Tim. 2:1–2 RSV)

We cannot be like the Lord, we cannot evangelize, and we cannot be salt for the earth if we are not walking in faithful obedience to Him.

I would like to leave you with an exhortation from Philippians: "Do everything without complaining or arguing, so that you may become blameless and pure, children of God without fault in a crooked and depraved generation, in which you shine like stars in the universe as you hold out the word of life—in order that I may boast on the day of Christ that I did not run or labor for nothing" (Phil. 2:14–16).

CHAPTER 4

ROMANS 7

*And so Jesus also suffered outside the city gate to make
the people holy through his own blood. (Heb. 13:12)*

In this chapter I will address a portion of Scripture which
many Christians would say contradicts the view of the
new nature and obedience that I am presenting in this
book. Romans 7 is often considered evidence that the
Apostle Paul had a real problem with obedience. If he did
indeed have such a problem, then of course it is under-
standable we should have one too. However, this was not
Paul's subject in that passage, and I will endeavor to make
clear what his subject was. Let's go through the chapter
verse by verse.

In Romans 7, Paul speaks to Christians who were well-acquainted with the Old Testament.

> Do you not know, brothers—*for I am speaking to men who know the law*—that the law has authority over man only as long as he lives? For example, by law, a married woman is bound to her husband as long as he is alive. But if her husband dies, she is released from the law of marriage. So then, if she marries another man while her husband is still alive, she is called an adulteress, but if her husband dies, she is released from that law and is not an adulteress, even though she marries another man. (Rom. 7:1–3)

A woman who becomes a widow is allowed to marry again, but she is not allowed to have two husbands at one time. Paul is not giving a lesson on marriage here. He is using an illustration from the Old Testament to teach this: "So, my brothers, *you also died to the law* through the body of Christ, that you might belong to another, to him who was raised from the dead, in order that we might bear fruit to God" (Rom. 7:4).

In Romans 6, Paul told the Roman Christians how they died to sin. In Romans 7, he explains that they have died to the law as well. When you were saved, you became a widow of the law. You are no longer married to it. *You died to the law through the body of Christ* at the same time that you died to sin. You have been properly widowed from sin and the law. Why? *That you might belong to another*—without committing bigamy.

Now you can belong to Him who was raised from the dead. Why are we married to Him? "In order that we might bear fruit to God. For when we were controlled by the sinful nature, the sinful passions aroused by the law were at work in our bodies so that we bore fruit for death" (Rom. 7:4b-5).

Some translations say "flesh" here (the literal translation), and some say "the sinful nature." The word "flesh" in this context does not refer to the physical body. Obviously Paul and the Romans still had physical bodies, or Paul couldn't have written the letter, and the Romans couldn't have read it. The "flesh" is the old nature.

"For when we were controlled by the sinful nature, the sinful passions aroused by the law were at work in our bodies, so that we bore fruit for death" (Rom. 7:5). When you were married to the law, the result was death. When you are married to Jesus Christ, the outcome is fruit for God.

Notice that in verse 5, Paul speaks in the past tense when he talks about being in the flesh: "while we *were* living in the flesh, our sinful passions...were at work." The structure of this sentence implies that "living in the flesh" is not something Paul is still doing, which means that *Paul is not in the flesh any longer.*

Paul also makes connections between "the flesh," "sinful passions," "the law," and "death." Flesh, law, sin, death: these four things are bound together in a tight cause-and-effect relationship in the natural man. Since Paul is no longer in the flesh, he is also not under the law, not bound by sin, and not in death. He was separated from all of that in Christ.

But when you were in the flesh and still attached to the law, your sinful passions were aroused by the law.[5] What does that mean?

The law provokes rebellion. Have you ever said to a child, "Johnny, don't touch Susie's toys"? What normally happens? Johnny goes around and touches every one of them, even if he had never thought of touching them before. That is the nature of sin. Once Johnny is told not to touch the toys, he suddenly wants to.

"But now, by dying to what once bound us, we have been released from the law so that we serve in the new way of the Spirit, and not in the old way of the written code" (Rom. 7:6). The sinful passions aroused by the law were causing us to bear fruit for death, *but now by* dying to *what once bound us*—by being widowed from the law—*we have been released from the law*. And we have been released from it *so that we may serve in the new way of the Spirit and not in the old way of the written code*. This is Paul's point: you cannot be married to more than one person at a time. You must die to the law *before* you can be married to Jesus Christ, because one bears fruit for death, and the other bears fruit to God.

In Romans 7:6, Paul makes a clear break. When we were under the law, our passions, sin, and death were in control. That is not the case anymore. We have been delivered from the law and, consequently, from death and the power of sin.

Paul had no difficulty making his point when he said that the flesh and sin and death went together—but by tying the

5 Here Paul is speaking primarily of the moral law, the Ten Commandments.

law to the other three, he knew he would be raising some questions. How can the good law be connected with sin? Paul knew the believers would be wondering this, so he anticipated their questions. *The rest of Romans 7 is Paul's explanation of the function of the law. That is all it is.*

Paul's first question is in verse 7, his second in verse 13. Verse 7 says, "What shall we say then? Is the law sin? Certainly not! Indeed I would not have known what sin was except through the law. For I would not have known what coveting really was if the law had not said, 'Do not covet'" (Rom. 7:7). Is the law sin? Of course not. God is not the author of sin.

In answering his own question, Paul goes into a first-person account, using his own past experience to describe the function of the law. He explains that the law was how he learned about what sin was. He would not have known he was a sinner if it had not been for the prohibitions of the law. "I *would not have known* what it was to covet if the law had not said, 'Do not covet'" (Rom. 7:7b).

The law is good because it tells you what sin is. Then Paul says something wonderful: "But sin, seizing the opportunity afforded by the commandment, produced in me every kind of covetous desire" (Rom. 7:8a).

When Paul learned that it was a sin to covet, there was a sin nature in him that sprang up and shouted, "Covet, covet, covet!" So the law defined sin, but the sin nature in Paul rebelled against the commandment of the law just like when I tell Johnny not to touch Susie's toys. Johnny's sin nature responds with, "Touch-touch-touch!"

"For apart from law, sin is dead" (Rom. 7:8b). If there were no law, sin would be powerless. Sin could not murder if there were no law that said, "You shall not murder." Sin could not steal if there were no law that said, "You shall not steal." Sin has no power without the command, for it is the nature of sin to *rebel*. Remember, Paul tells all of this in the first person singular and the past tense.

"Once I was alive apart from law; but when the commandment came, sin sprang to life and I died" (Rom. 7:9). Sometime in the past, Paul had been without the law. When could that have been? Before he first heard the commandment. In Acts 22:3, Paul testifies to his rearing in the "perfect law" in which he continued until he became "dead to the law" at his conversion, so the time "apart from the law" would have to have been in his infancy and early childhood. During that time, Paul says, he was spiritually "alive."

When the commandment came, sin awakened, and he died. This cannot be speaking of Paul's Christian life, for how could he die spiritually *after* becoming a Christian? It also could not have been right before his Christian life, because he says that right before conversion he was not spiritually alive, but *dead* in the sins the law had convicted him of. The only time Paul could have been alive apart from the law was sometime in his infancy.

This relates to original sin. If we say man is not naturally sinful, we have a real problem to explain. Suppose man were born inherently good. Then the overwhelming majority of the seven billion people on earth should be good. If they started out neutral (neither good nor bad) then we should have three and a half billion good people and three and a half billion bad people. But we are not coming out that well. The only good explanation for why 100% of people turn out bad is that we all started out with the tendency to sin.

Paul says that even with that tendency, he was alive—until the commandment came. Then there was a transition from life to death. Sin had been there all along, but it was dormant. Then it awakened. The commandment allowed Paul's sin tendency to come to life and covet—and when it did, he died. After that, by actually practicing sin, he was spiritually dead and in need of salvation through Christ.

Paul states a contradiction in verse 10: "I found that the very commandment that was intended to bring life actually brought death."

How? "*For sin*, seizing the opportunity afforded by the commandment, deceived me, and through the commandment, *put me to death*" (Rom. 7:11).

Sin deceives as Satan did in the Garden—starting with a commandment. Sin is the cause of death. The law itself is holy, but the rebellious nature needs a command to rebel against.

I knew a trumpet player in the Naval Academy band who used to moonlight in nightclubs playing the piano to make extra money. One night, he took his wife with him. She was a beautiful woman. She sat by the piano while he played. At one point, she excused herself and went to the ladies' room. While she was gone, he looked around the room and saw a beautiful woman out of the corner of his eye. He thought, "What a dish." He turned to take another look and said, "Oh, it's my wife." All of a sudden, the great attraction was gone.

That was not just biology. She was the same beautiful woman after he recognized her. It was the prohibition that made her look so good when he did not know who she was. The Scripture says, "Stolen waters are sweet, and bread eaten in secret is pleasant" (Prov. 9:17 kjv).

Romans 7:12 repeats Paul's statement of the innocence of the law, despite its connection with the evils of the flesh, sin, and death: "So then, the law is holy, and the commandment is holy, righteous and good."

In verse 13, Paul asks his second question: "Did that which is good, then, become death to me?"

· Before we look at his answer, note that Paul is still very clearly speaking of himself when he was not a Christian. The verb is in the past tense, and sin and death are repeated five times. Paul has told how sin takes advantage of the law, and now he tells how the law shows up sin for its real character: "Did that which is good, then, become death to me? By no means. But *in order that sin might be recognized as sin,* it produced death in me through what was good, so that through the commandment, sin might become utterly sinful" (Rom. 7:13).

The purpose of the law is to make sin *recognizable.* But at the same time, sin rebels against it, causing death. In other words, we do *not* die because of the Ten Commandments. We do *not* die because we have not heard of Jesus Christ. We die because of *sin.* "The day that you eat of the fruit of the tree in the middle of the garden, you will die."[6] It is a good commandment and a rebellious sin.

Besides being holy and just and good, the law is also spiritual: "We know that the law is spiritual; but I am unspiritual, sold as a slave to sin" (Rom. 7:14).

This is the problem verse. In verses 9–11, the Apostle Paul (first person, past tense) died, and he is still dead in verse 13. But verse 14 is in the present tense. Because it is in the present tense, some Christians think that the Apostle Paul had the problem he wrote about here *as a Christian.* Consequently, they use this Scripture as a means of justifying sin in their own lives.

But we just left the Apostle Paul *dead in sin* in verse 13. If Paul were writing about his current problems, he would have had to either change the subject or mention his conversion between verses 13 and 14, and he does *neither.* Verse 14: "But we know that the law is spiritual." He is still on the same subject, the nature of the law. He is not converted, either, because he says, "I am *unspiritual,* sold as *a slave to sin.*"

In Romans 6, Paul made a major case that we *used to be* slaves to sin, and we were set free from that in Christ. So when he says, "I am unspiritual, sold as a slave to sin," did he get back under that slavery again between writing Romans 6 and Romans 7? No! Is he a slave to sin as a believer? No!

In Romans 7:14, Paul is employing what is called the *historic present*—using the present tense to draw a vivid picture of the past, making it seem like it is happening right

6 See Genesis 2:17.

now. Why would Paul use the historic present? To illustrate the state of death. "This is how I *died* (verses 7 and 8)... Now this *is* death." That is why he changes tenses.

Verse 14 cannot be speaking of Paul as a Christian. His declaration, "I am unspiritual, sold as a slave to sin," is a strong statement for a Christian to make at any time, but especially right after the freedom Paul spoke about in Romans 6. Moreover, Paul's state gets even worse as we keep reading: "I do not understand what I do. For what I want to do, I do not do, but what I hate, I do" (Rom. 7:15).

Many Christians might say, "Yeah, that describes me." But even if it does describe you, it certainly did not describe the converted Apostle Paul. He knew what he was doing, and we can see from his other teachings that he had this authority and power.

However, even if Paul had been speaking of himself as a Christian in verse 14, since when are we to look to Paul? We are not to get our examples from anyone in defeat. "Therefore, since we are surrounded by so great a cloud of witnesses, let us also lay aside every weight, and sin which clings so closely, and let us run with perseverance the race that is set before us, *looking to Jesus, the pioneer and perfecter of our faith*" (Heb. 12:1–2 RSV). If you want to use Paul as an example, use him in his *victory*, not in his defeat. No matter how you look at it, Romans 7 provides no rationalization for sin in the Christian life.

In this passage, Paul is giving an assessment of his state as a *natural man*. Verses 7–13 tell us how Paul died, and verses 14–24 describe the unsaved man's state of spiritual death.

"I do not understand what I do. For what I want to do I do not do, but what I hate I do. And if I do what I do not want to do, I agree that the law is good" (Rom. 7:15–16). This man cannot be good when he chooses to be and cannot keep from being bad when he chooses not to be. He is in an impossible situation. Here is Paul, a natural man with inherent knowledge of good and evil, educated in God's revelation from early childhood, and agreeing that the law is good. He finds himself looking for an explanation for:

1. Wanting good and not doing it
2. Hating evil and doing it

He gives the reason in verse 17: "As it is, it is no longer I myself who do it, but it is sin living in me.

Over the years, many people have come to me and said, "Jim, I don't know why I sin; I know the difference between right and wrong."

I say, "That's the reason."

"What is?"

"You know the difference." When the Apostle Paul learned the difference between good and evil, what did he do? He *sinned*. Do you remember the name of that tree in the Garden of Eden? The Tree of *the Knowledge of Good and Evil*. Eating from it had a consequence—the tendency to be evil. *Knowing the difference between right and wrong comes with a tendency to do wrong.* People think that if we all just knew the difference between right and wrong, of course we would choose to do right.

Then why don't we? "I know that nothing good lives in me, that is, in my sinful nature. For I have the desire to do what is good, but I cannot carry it out" (Rom. 7:18).

Plenty of unbelievers desire to be good, especially those who know the law. I certainly did before I was a Christian. I really worked at it—but it was hopeless. "For what I do is not the good I want to do; no, the evil I do not want to do—this I keep on doing" (Rom. 7:19).

The natural man retains only enough will to make a decision for good: "For I have the desire to do what is good, but I cannot carry it out" (Rom. 7:18b). He can choose to do good, but because of his sin he has no power to back up the decision. Just as the law was not the cause of the disobedience, neither can it *cause* obedience. The law is like a speed-limit sign on the highway. It does not make us obey the speed limit: it only brings that limit to our attention.

"Now if I do what I do not want to do, it is no longer I who do it, but it is sin living in me that does it" (Rom. 7:20). Christians, you may think this describes you. You may be all messed up. But if you are, it is for another reason. Whether Paul is speaking in this chapter about himself as a Christian or as a natural man, one thing is clear: this person is incapable of obeying God and incapable of not disobeying God. Other Scripture clearly makes such a state untrue of Christians:

> No temptation has seized you except what is common to man. *And God is faithful; he will not let you be tempted beyond what you can bear.* But when you are tempted, he will also provide a way out so that you can stand up under it. (1 Cor. 10:13)

> My dear children, I write this to you *so that you will not sin*. But if anybody does sin, we have one who speaks to the Father in our defense—Jesus Christ, the Righteous One. He is the atoning sacrifice for our sins, and not only for ours but also for the sins of the whole world. (1 John 2:1–2)

> I put this in human terms because you are weak in your natural selves. Just as you used to offer the parts of your body in slavery to impurity and to ever-increasing wickedness, so now *offer them in slavery to righteousness leading to holiness.* (Rom. 6:19)

This passage must be speaking of someone who is not yet a Christian—that is, Paul before his conversion. "So I find this law at work: When I want to do good, evil is right there with me. For in my inner being I delight in God's law; but I see another law at work in the members of my body, waging war against the law of my mind and making me a prisoner of *the law of sin* at work within my members" (Rom. 7:21–23). I don't want to commit murder or adultery; I delight in the standard. "But I see another law at work in the members of my body, waging war against the law of my mind and making me a prisoner of the law of sin at work within my members." That is the key phrase: the law of sin. The law of God is a standard, and the law of sin is a power.

Before his conversion, Paul was a religious man, much more educated in morality than people of western culture are today. He delighted in the law of God (as I did in my youth, and as many others have); but he saw another law more powerful, winning over the law of his mind (that is, his education) and winning over the "law of God after the inward man" (his inherent knowledge of the moral law). The moral law has no power. The law of sin *does* have power, and it enslaves. Paul finds himself a captive to it. He wants to be good, and he cannot be. What a frustration!

Paul cries out in his testimony, "What a wretched man I am! Who will rescue me from this body of death?" (Rom. 7:24).

The answer: "Thanks be to God—through *Jesus Christ our Lord!*" (Rom. 7:25a).

There is his conversion. Paul was a slave to the law of sin, and Jesus Christ set him free. This is very important. In Romans 8, Paul continues his statement of deliverance. Romans 8 is not speaking of the victorious Christian as opposed to the defeated Christian of Romans 7. Romans 7 is about the helpless state of the non-Christian man.

"There is therefore now no condemnation for those who are in Christ Jesus. For *the law of the Spirit of life in Christ Jesus has set me free* from the law of sin and death" (Rom. 8:1–2 RSV). "There is…no condemnation." Paul does not say "no defeat." He is talking about *basic salvation* here. There is no condemnation for those who are in Christ. If you are in Christ, the law of the spirit of life has set you free from the law of sin and death.

"For what the law was powerless to do in that it was weakened by the sinful nature, God did by sending his own Son in the likeness of sinful man to be a sin offering. And so he condemned sin in sinful man, in order that the righteous requirements of the law might be fully met in us, who do not live according to the sinful nature but according to the Spirit" (Rom. 8:3–4). Romans 7 was all death and slavery. Romans 8 proclaims freedom for those who are in *Christ*. When I was under the law, I could not meet its requirements because the law of sin had brought me into captivity. When Jesus Christ became a sin offering, He condemned the sin that held me in bondage, in order that I could be obedient. If I know the Ten Commandments before I am a Christian, I have no power to obey them. After I have received Jesus Christ, I can obey them fully. Although the moral law does not change, our *ability* to live it changes, just by being in Jesus Christ.

"Those who live according to the sinful nature have their minds set on what that nature desires, but those who live in accordance with the Spirit have their minds set on what the Spirit desires" (Rom. 8:5). These desires do not coexist. It is an either-or situation.

"The mind of sinful man is death, but the mind controlled by the Spirit is life and peace; the sinful mind is hostile to God. It does not submit to God's law, nor can it do so. *Those controlled by the sinful nature cannot please God. You, however, are controlled not by the sinful nature but by the Spirit*, if the Spirit of God lives in you. And if anyone does not have the Spirit of Christ, he does not belong to Christ" (Rom. 8:6–9). Why do you sin? For one of two reasons:

1. You are not dead to sin; you are still married to the law. You are in captivity to that sin which reigns in your members so that you cannot please God, no

matter how hard you try. If Romans 7 describes you very well, it is likely that you are not a Christian.

2. You have chosen to sin. It is not that you cannot avoid sin, but that you will not. If you know that you are saved and you are sinning, it is simply choice. You do not have to. The provision of preventative grace is there in the Cross.

Galatians 5 contains another "problem verse" similar to Romans 7:14. "For the sinful nature desires what is contrary to the spirit and the spirit what is contrary to the sinful nature. They are in conflict with each other so that you do not do what you want" (Gal. 5:17). This verse is a parallel to the Romans 7 passage where the law of sin is in control. "But if you are led by the Spirit, you are not under law" (Gal. 5:18). The issue is the same—not being under the law if you are led by the Spirit.

> The acts of the sinful nature are obvious: sexual immorality, impurity and debauchery; idolatry and witchcraft; hatred, discord, jealousy, fits of rage, selfish ambition, dissensions, factions and envy; drunkenness, orgies, and the like. I warn you, as I did before, that those who live like this will not inherit the kingdom of God. (Gal. 5:19–21)

> But the fruit of the Spirit is love, joy, peace, patience, kindness, goodness, faithfulness, gentleness and self-control. Against such things there is no law. Those who belong to Christ Jesus have crucified the sinful nature with its passions and desires. (Gal. 5:22–24)

Those in the first list will not inherit the kingdom of God. If you are in the second, if you belong to Christ, you have crucified the flesh with its passions and desires.

The difference between an unbeliever's sin and a believer's sin is like the difference between a bobsled and a pogo stick. An unbeliever bobsleds in sin, and a Christian pogo-sticks into it. The unbeliever has continual contact with sin. The Christian just touches into it here and there. Unfortunately, some Christians are pogo-sticking so fast it looks like they have continual contact with the ground. (Of course, my analogy falls short because gravity has to pull the pogo stick down again, and there is no reason for that to happen in the Christian life.)

Twenty to forty percent of the people in the United States claim to be born-again believers. That is at least sixty million people. I believe it is a high estimate, not because these people have not had some sort of born-again experience, but because their lives have not changed. They do not live like they are in the second list.

Can't I be in both lists? Yes, but if you are a Christian and you are in the first one, it is by your choice, and it is sin. Get out of it today. Get out of it now. It is unnatural for you to live that way. You live by the Spirit. If you are in the first list and you cannot do the good that you want to do, you are not a believer. You may be a believer in your head, but your life and your heart have not changed.

CHAPTER 5

RIGHTEOUSNESS
AND HOLINESS

Follow peace with all men, and holiness, without
which no man shall see the Lord. (Heb. 12:14 KJV)

We are to serve God with both holiness and righteousness. Jesus enables us to do this all our days. "Praise
be to the Lord, the God of Israel, because he has come and
has redeemed his people. He has raised up a horn of salvation for us in the house of his servant David...to enable
us to serve him without fear in holiness and righteousness
before him all our days" (Luke 1:68–69, 74b-75).

Righteousness is impurity that has been made clean. It
means our sins have been forgiven.

> For in the gospel a righteousness from God is re-vealed, a righteousness that is by faith from first to last, just as it is written: "The righteous will live by faith." (Rom. 1:17)

> But now a righteousness from God, apart from law, has been made known, to which the Law and the Prophets testify. This righteousness from God comes through faith in Jesus Christ to all who believe. (Rom. 3:21–22a)

> This is why "it was credited to him as righteous-ness." The words "it was credited to him" were writ-ten not for him alone, but also for us, to whom God will credit righteousness—for us who believe in him who raised Jesus our Lord from the dead. He was delivered over to death for our sins and was raised to life for our justification. (Rom. 4:22–25)

> Brothers, my heart's desire and prayer to God for the Israelites is that they may be saved. For I can testify about them that they are zealous for God, but their zeal is not based on knowledge. Since they did not know the righteousness that comes from God and sought to establish their own, they did not submit to God's righteousness. Christ is the end of the law so that there may be righteousness for everyone who believes. (Rom. 10:1–4)

Righteousness is from God. It comes to us through the gospel which we receive by faith. We have no righteous-ness of our own. Now we are washed, cleaned, and dressed in God's righteousness.

God's righteousness imparted to us is the starting point of the Christian life. Being made clean makes it possible to obey God, which is holiness.

> I put this in human terms because you are weak in your natural selves. Just as you used to offer the parts of your body in slavery to impurity and to ever-increasing wickedness, so now offer them in slavery to righteousness leading to holiness. (Rom. 6:19)

> But now that you have been set free from sin and have become slaves to God, the benefit you reap leads to holiness, and the result is eternal life. (Rom. 6:22)

Holiness has two parts:

1. Obeying the prohibitions, i.e., not getting dirty. "And so he condemned sin in sinful man, in order that the righteous requirements of the law might be fully met in us, who do not live according to the sinful nature but according to the Spirit" (Rom. 8:3b–4).
2. Obeying the positive commands with joy (e.g., love your enemy, rejoice always, pray without ceasing, in everything give thanks, forgive your brother from your heart). "Therefore, I urge you, brothers, in view of God's mercy, to offer your bodies as living sacrifices, holy and pleasing to God—this is your spiritual act of worship. Do not conform any longer to the pattern of this world, but be transformed by the renewing of your mind. Then you will be able to test and approve what God's will is—his good, pleasing and perfect will" (Rom. 12:1–2).

Notice that our bodies are to be holy and pleasing to God. We are to be more than just clean. "And we, who with unveiled faces all *reflect the Lord's glory,* are *being transformed into his likeness* with ever-increasing glory, which comes from the Lord, who is the Spirit" (2 Cor. 3:18).

In Philippians, Paul speaks of his righteousness and his growing holiness.

His righteousness:

> What is more, I consider everything a loss compared to the surpassing greatness of knowing Christ Jesus my Lord, for whose sake I have lost all things. I consider them rubbish, that I may gain Christ and be found in him, not having a righteousness of my own that comes from the law, but that which is through faith in Christ—the righteousness that comes from God and is by faith. (Phil. 3:8–9)

His holiness:

> I want to know Christ and the power of his resurrection and the fellowship of sharing in his sufferings, becoming like him in his death, and so, somehow, to attain to the resurrection from the dead. Not that I have already obtained all this, or have already been made perfect, but I press on to take hold of that for which Christ Jesus took hold of me. Brothers, I do not consider myself yet to have taken hold of it. But one thing I do: Forgetting what is behind and straining toward what is ahead, I press on toward the goal to win the prize for which God has called me heavenward in Christ Jesus. (Phil. 3:10–14)

Most Christians are content with just staying righteous. Many of them do not succeed even there. Very few want to be holy.

CHAPTER 6

OBEDIENCE
IS NORMAL

For God did not call us to be impure,
but to live a holy life. (1 Thess. 4:7)

There are at least two different definitions of "normal life": God's definition and man's. Man defines normal as what is average. God's definition is far above average. This chapter is not about the average Christian life. It is about what the Christian life should be—holiness.

If we took a survey of Christians today, we could not honestly say that obedience to God is the norm. And yet it is God's expectation. Obedience really is the *normal* state for Christians.

There is no place for sin in the Christian life. Because God took care of everything at the cross, He expects you to be fully obedient from the time you are born again. Really? Yes, *really*.

Imagine you are a brand-new Christian. You ask the person who led you to Christ if you are supposed to obey all the time, and he says, "Well, no; you have to grow into obedience."

"All right, how should I do it?"

He says, "Let's take the Ten Commandments and make a ten-year plan for your obedience."

"Ok, sounds good. So this year, I will not commit adultery. Next year, I will not commit adultery or murder. The third year, I will quit bearing false witness. After that, I will stop stealing. In ten years, I'll be a perfect Christian."

Are you laughing right now? I hope so, because that is ridiculous! *Of course* you are expected to be completely obedient from the time you are converted!

"My little children, these things write I unto you, that ye *sin not*. And if any man sin, we have an advocate with the Father, Jesus Christ the righteous: And he is the propitiation for our sins: and not for ours only, but also for the sins of the whole world" (1 John 2:1–2 KJV). If we sin, we have an advocate with the Father. That is true, but the basic sentence in this verse is *do not sin*. Do not rely on the provision for sin and forget the command! Where does the Bible tell us to sin? It tells us *not to*.

The law requires obedience, which God provided for through Jesus' death and resurrection. (The change was in *us*, not in the Ten Commandments.[7] After I received Christ, it did not suddenly become right to commit adultery.) If you are a Christian, you can keep the law now, although that law is still the same. It is no longer normal to go touch Susie's toys when you are told not to. Because of God's actions of grace on our behalf, it is both possible and *normal* to obey.

> Do not lie to each other, since *you have taken off your*
> *old self with its practices and have put on the new self*,
> which is being renewed in knowledge in the image
> of its Creator. (Col. 3:9–10)

The command "Do not lie to each other" implies that it is possible to lie. That might seem obvious. The reason I point it out is that by the end of this chapter you might think that I am saying it is impossible to lie. I want to make it plain from the start that I am agreeing with the text. Christians have the *ability* to lie to each other, and we are not supposed to do it.

There are several ways of looking at the Bible. One of them is from your previous teaching (i.e., Sunday school, denominational background, church background, family background). What we should always do is look at the Scriptures fresh. Do not expect them to concur with your previous Sunday school teaching. If you do, you may wind up making the Bible fit your preconceived notions rather than seeing what it really says. We all come from different

7 The terms "Ten Commandments," "law," and "moral law" are used interchangeably in this book. The Ten Commandments are the law that governs our morality, our behavior towards God and others.

denominations and backgrounds, and the Scriptures certainly cannot agree with all of them. So enter the Bible fresh. Don't expect it to rubber-stamp your previous doctrine.

Second, do not look at the Scriptures in the light of your experience. When I teach, I tell many stories to illustrate my points, but I do not teach experientially. I get my teaching from the Bible. Interpreting the Bible through your experiences is like having colored glasses on. You make the text conform to you; you read things into it that are not biblical. For instance, there are Christians who are depressed. When they read Scripture, it does not pull them out of depression. Since their experience is depressing, what they see on every page are more reasons to be depressed. Reading the Bible with the colored glasses of their depression blinds them to the truth of Scripture.

Consider someone who is defeated. When he reads the Scripture, does he find verses to bring him out of defeat? No. He looks for an *explanation* for why he is defeated, not a *solution* to the defeat. How about someone who has just spoken in tongues? What does he see in Scripture? Suddenly the whole Bible is talking about speaking in tongues! Speaking in tongues is in Scripture, but there is also much more there, and he tends to miss it. This is not right. Explain your experiences from the text, not the text from your experiences. The Bible is always much bigger than our experience. When we read it with colored glasses on, we miss much, and we misinterpret much.

I am not the only one that teaches this, but there are very few people that emphasize it today because it has become normal to interpret Scripture in the light of our own experiences. Often people don't even know they are doing it. We must take the glasses off and see the Scripture starkly. One of the things we need to see is that *it is normal to obey*. You say, "Not with me." Stop: you have just interpreted Scripture in the light of your experience. Believe me: *the Bible says it is normal to obey*. Start with that.

If we judge the verses we have read in the light of our experiences, we might think that the Scriptures are overstated. We might say, "The Christian life cannot be like that, because I have not experienced it, and I do not know anyone else who has experienced it. These statements must be idealistic goals which we should strive for but which we will not attain until we go to be with the Lord." We do not attain to these things: they just *are*. The Scriptures I have quoted are all about what *Christ has done* for us.

Do not reduce the Scripture to what you think your ability is. Read the Scriptures as they are. If we do this, every one of us will change. Every one of us. Do not read them in the light of your experience. Do not even read them in the light of my teaching. Your responsibility is to seek it out for yourself. "As soon as it was night, the brothers sent Paul and Silas away to Berea. On arriving there, they went to the Jewish synagogue. Now *the Bereans were of more noble character* than the Thessalonians, *for they* received the message with great eagerness and *examined the Scriptures every day to see if what Paul said was true*" (Acts 17:10–11).

Christ has made absolute obedience possible by what He did for us.

"I have been *crucified with Christ* and I no longer live, but *Christ lives in me.* The life I now live in the body, *I live by faith in the Son of God, who loved me and gave himself for me.* I do not set aside the grace of God, for if righteousness could be gained through the law, Christ died for nothing!" (Gal. 2:20–21). Amen. The old man is dead and gone. Do not listen to the lies of the devil who says we have to keep on sinning. Our world is sovereignly controlled by God, but within it Satan has much freedom, and he takes it. Deception is his most powerful tool.

"For such men are false apostles, deceitful workmen, masquerading as apostles of Christ" (2 Cor. 11:13). These people pretend to be apostles of Christ. We should not be surprised at this. "And no wonder, for Satan himself masquerades as an angel of light. It is not surprising, then, if his servants masquerade as servants of righteousness. Their end will be what their actions deserve" (2 Cor. 11:14–15).

Many people masquerade as apostles of Christ. Some are even the devil's servants without knowing it. Unfortunately, the wolf in sheep's clothing does not announce, "I am a wolf. I came here to eat you; don't pay attention to this sheep's clothing." He says, "I am a sheep." Similarly, a false prophet does not say, "I am lying; do not listen to me." He says, "I am speaking the truth." But that is also what the true prophets say. We need to know who is really telling the truth and who is not. In order to see through the Enemy's deception, we have to be spiritually alert. We need to know the Book.

Most people who masquerade like this are not very good at it, but, sadly, they do not have to be, because the

Christians cannot tell the difference. If an angel came through your ceiling right now, shining like lightning, you might be tempted to assume he came from God. But he may not have. Something being miraculous does not prove it is of God. The way to know if it is from God is to check what the angel says against the Bible. If his words do not fit the Bible's, he is lying. Many books in print now tell stories of miracles and of having seen angels, but they do not conform to Scripture. The teaching is wrong, but people who want to believe the miracle buy the book anyway. They have chosen to follow the world.

This deception comes outside religion as well. The television and the internet lie to us all day long. So do our classmates, our professors. "You mean they're lying?" Well, perhaps not maliciously, but they are living in a system that is a lie. If we allow ourselves to grow accustomed to this system, we begin to think like it and wind up going happily along for the ride. As Christians, we do not have to, we should not, and we must not go along with it.

I am not saying that we need to stand apart from all the activities of the world. After all, the Lord Jesus told us we are to be *in* the world—just not *of* it. Be in the world, but keep in mind that if you do not pay attention to what is happening around you, you will soon be following the world, and you will be doing it by your own choice.

I will say it again: once I am a Christian, my sin is a *choice*. I sin because I decide to, but often I decide because I have been lied to. *It is our business to tell the difference between Satan's lies and God's truth, and the way to do that is by reading the Word of God. Some options are obviously straight from the other team, but Christians give them equal weight because they do not know their God. They believe the devil's caricature of Him because they are not steeped in the Word. Not knowing the Bible sets you up to fall when temptation comes along.

> Therefore, if anyone is in Christ, he is a new creation; the old has gone, the new has come! (2 Cor. 5:17)

Every man in Christ is a new creature. The old things have passed away; *all things* have become new.

> You, however, are controlled not by the sinful nature but by the Spirit, if the Spirit of God lives in you. And if anyone does not have the Spirit of Christ, he does not belong to Christ. (Rom. 8:9)

If the Spirit of God dwells in you, you are in the Spirit. Since we are in the Spirit, what are we to do?

> Therefore do not let sin reign in your mortal body so that you obey its evil desires. Do not offer the parts of your body to sin… (Rom. 6:12–13)

Again, offering your body to sin is a *choice*. "But I don't make a conscious choice; I just sin." If this is true, you might just be making fast decisions. That is what habits are. You have made them so often that you don't even think about them.

You must not choose this. Christ did not tell you not to sin, knowing you cannot help it. He told you not to sin because He has provided the means for you not to. He means you to live a victorious, obedient life, and *He* provides the power for you to do it.

I will give you five sentences about Christians. Three of them are true, and two of them are false. Answer them in your head as you read. I do not want you to answer them experientially; I want you to answer *biblically*. Here they are:

1. *It is possible to sin.* True. Because the Bible commands us not to sin, sin must be possible—otherwise the command would not have been necessary.

2. *It is impossible to sin.* False. This cannot be true, since 1 was true.

3. *It is impossible not to sin.* This is the difficult one. Many Christians believe it is true. But it is a double negative; it is simply saying, "You must sin." That is false. The Bible says you must *not* sin.

4. *It is possible not to sin.* True, or God would not have told us not to.

5. *It is impossible to live in sin.* True.

> No one who lives in him keeps on sinning. No one who continues to sin has either seen him or known him... No one who is born of God will continue to sin, because God's seed remains in him; he cannot go on sinning, because he has been born of God. (1 John 3:6, 9)

> We know that anyone born of God does not continue to sin; the one who was born of God keeps him safe, and the evil one cannot harm him. (1 John 5:18)

Remember that at the beginning of the chapter, I wanted you to be careful about what I was saying. *I am not saying it is impossible to sin as a Christian.* I am saying *it is possible not to sin,* and that God made it possible by dying to sin on the cross. 1 Peter 2:24a: "He Himself bore our sins in His body on the tree."

The sin Christ died to was sin itself in all its power, not just sin symptoms. When you take care of the disease, you take care of the symptoms, too. Have you ever been around unbelievers who decided to quit swearing? How did they do? Probably not very well, right? But if they become Christians, what happens to the profanity? They say one bad word and want to bite their tongues. They feel guilty like they never felt guilty when they were not believers. When their sin disease was taken care of, the symptoms (the swearing) went with it.

This happened to us when we became Christians, and we know it. However, some of us have believed Satan's lie that we still have to act like we used to act in some ways: we still have those "problem areas" that we can't get rid of. No, we do not. God gives grace to prevent this. "For sin shall not be your master, because you are not under law, but under grace" (Rom. 6:14). You are under grace, and grace means power over sin.

> What then? Shall we sin because we are not under law but under grace? By no means! Don't you know that when you offer yourself to someone to obey him as slaves, you are slaves to the one whom you obey—whether you are a slave to sin, which leads to death, or to obedience, which leads to righteousness? Thanks be to God that, though you used to be

slaves to sin, you wholeheartedly obeyed the former teaching to which you were entrusted. *You have been set free from sin and have become slaves to righteousness.* (Rom. 6:15–18)

Through the death of Jesus Christ, you have become slaves to righteousness. You do not need any other experience to give you victory over sin than simply passing from death to life by believing on Him.

"I put this in human terms because you are weak in your natural selves. Just as you used to offer the parts of your body in slavery to impurity and ever-increasing wickedness, so now offer them in slavery to righteousness leading to holiness" (Rom. 6:19). The old man sins to ever-increasing wickedness; the new man starts out in righteousness leading to ever-increasing holiness.

You may say, "But if you did not have the old nature anymore, then you wouldn't sin; you would be automatically holy." That is not what the Bible says. According to Scripture, you made a basic choice to follow Christ, and you keep on making choices now.

"When you were slaves to sin, you were free from the control of righteousness. What benefit did you reap at that time from the things you are now ashamed of?" (Rom. 6:20–21a). You did not reap any benefit. "Those things result in death! But now that you have been set free from sin and have become slaves to God, the benefit you reap leads to holiness, and the result is eternal life" (Rom. 6:21b-22).

Your salvation alone makes that difference. Many evangelicals emphasize the new birth but think they need another experience to make them victorious. When we look for a second experience, we are becoming man-centered instead of God-centered. Don't look for another experience: look to Jesus. "Let us fix our eyes on Jesus, the author and perfecter of our faith, who for the joy set before him endured the cross, scorning its shame, and sat down at the right hand of the throne of God" (Heb. 12:2).

Jesus Christ provided for everything—forgiveness, holiness, and everlasting life—at the same time. "Since, then, you have been raised with Christ, set your hearts on things above, where Christ is seated at the right hand of God. Set your minds on things above, not on earthly things. For you died, and your life is now hidden with Christ in God. When Christ, who is your life, appears, then you also will appear with him in glory. Put to death, therefore, whatever belongs to your earthly nature" (Col. 3:1–5a).

Think back on the five sentences discussed earlier. If you are a Christian, three things are true for you: it is possible to sin, it is possible not to sin, and it is impossible to live in sin. The other two are false.

We were created in the image of God with free will. By definition, free will is independent of both the old nature and the new. However, our free will became enslaved to the old nature before we were saved. It is enslaved no longer.

There is a difference between wanting or deciding to do something and actually performing the action you willed to do. In Romans 7, Paul says that when we were non-Christians, we could will to do what was right, but could not do it. That is because of the law of sin. A Christian can will and do, but a non-Christian can only will; he cannot produce.

The old nature enslaves. The Holy Spirit leaves us free. A Christian has freedom to disobey more than a non-Christian has freedom to obey. This is the nature of God. He will not make us robots. He brings us back into liberty. We can use that liberty to sin, or we can use that liberty to obey God. Do not use it as an occasion for the flesh.

"Put to death, therefore whatever belongs to your earthly nature: sexual immorality, impurity, lust, evil desires and greed, which is idolatry" (Col. 3:5). Paul told the Colossian Christians to put these things to death. Any Christian can have problems with these. What is important to grasp from this verse is that these sins *can* and *should* be put to death. Putting something to death is not a slow process. It is an immediate event.

"Because of these, the wrath of God is coming" (Col. 3:6). These sins are bringing everlasting judgment upon non-Christians. In these, Paul says, you once lived normally (Col. 3:7). Once upon a time, this was natural—but now, put them all away. You are no longer in slavery to sin. "But thanks be to God, who gives us the victory through our Lord Jesus Christ" (1 Cor. 15:57 RSV).

CHAPTER 7

THE HOLY SPIRIT

But you, dear friends, build yourselves up in your most
holy faith and pray in the Holy Spirit. (Jude 20)

When we received Christ, we were born from above and became part of the body of Christ.

> Yet to all who received him, to those who believed in his name, he gave the right to become children of God—children born not of natural descent, nor of human decision or a husband's will, but born of God. (John 1:12–13)

> For we were all baptized by one Spirit into one body—whether Jews or Greeks, slave or free—and we were all given the one Spirit to drink. (1 Cor. 12:13)

When we received Christ, we were also marked with the Holy Spirit, guaranteeing our inheritance of eternal life, and we received the fruit of the Spirit.

> Now it is God who makes both us and you stand firm in Christ. He anointed us, set his seal of ownership on us, and put his Spirit in our hearts as a deposit, guaranteeing what is to come. (2 Cor. 1:21–22)

> And you also were included in Christ when you heard the word of truth, the gospel of your salvation. Having believed, you were marked in him with a seal, the promised Holy Spirit. (Eph. 1:13)

> But the fruit of the Spirit is love, joy, peace, patience, kindness, goodness, faithfulness, gentleness and self-control. Against such things there is no law. (Gal. 5:22–23)

God gives us wisdom and great power through His Spirit.

> I keep asking that the God of our Lord Jesus Christ, the glorious Father, may give you the Spirit of wisdom and revelation, so that you may know him better. I pray also that the eyes of your heart may be enlightened in order that you may know the hope to which he has called you, the riches of his glorious inheritance in the saints, and his incomparably great power for us who believe. That power is like the working of his mighty strength, which he exerted in Christ when he raised him from the dead and seated him at his right hand in the heavenly realms, far above all rule and authority, power and dominion,

and every title that can be given, not only in the present age but also in the one to come. (Eph. 1:17–21)

When filled with the Spirit, we receive boldness to preach the gospel.

All of them were filled with the Holy Spirit and began to speak in other tongues as the Spirit enabled them. (Acts 2:4)

After they prayed, the place where they were meeting was shaken. And they were all filled with the Holy Spirit and spoke the word of God boldly. (Acts 4:31)

"Brothers, choose seven men from among you who are known to be full of the Spirit and wisdom. We will turn this responsibility over to them and will give our attention to prayer and the ministry of the word."…Now Stephen, a man full of God's grace and power, did great wonders and miraculous signs among the people. (Acts 6:3–4, 8)

We are sons of God and heirs with Christ.

For if you live according to the sinful nature, you will die; but if by the Spirit you put to death the misdeeds of the body, you will live, because those who are led by the Spirit of God are sons of God. For you did not receive a spirit that makes you a slave again to fear, but you received the Spirit of sonship. And by him we cry, "Abba, Father." The Spirit himself testifies with our spirit that we are God's children. Now if we are children, then we are heirs—heirs of God and

> co-heirs with Christ, if indeed we share in his suf-
> ferings in order that we may also share in his glory.
> (Rom. 8:13–17)

When we live by the Spirit, we will not glorify the desires of the flesh. "So I say, live by the Spirit, and you will not gratify the desires of the sinful nature...Since we live by the Spirit, let us keep in step with the Spirit" (Gal. 5:16, 25).

The Holy Spirit teaches us and guides us into truth.

> But the Counselor, the Holy Spirit, whom the Father
> will send in my name, will teach you all things and
> will remind you of everything I have said to you.
> (John 14:26)

> But when he, the Spirit of truth, comes, he will guide
> you into all truth. He will not speak on his own; he
> will speak only what he hears, and he will tell you
> what is yet to come. (John 16:13)

The Holy Spirit continues to grow us into Christlikeness. "And we, who with unveiled faces all reflect the Lord's glory, are being transformed into his likeness with ever-increasing glory, which comes from the Lord, who is the Spirit" (2 Cor. 3:18).

We are to keep on being filled with the Spirit.

> Do not get drunk on wine, which leads to debauch-
> ery. Instead, be filled with the Spirit. Speak to one
> another with psalms, hymns and spiritual songs.
> Sing and make music in your heart to the Lord, al-
> ways giving thanks to God the Father for everything,
> in the name of our Lord Jesus Christ. (Eph. 5:18–20)

Obedience is evidence of our life in the Spirit. "Those who obey his commands live in him, and he in them. And this is how we know that he lives in us: We know it by the Spirit he gave us" (1 John 3:24).

These are not the only Scriptures that tell us of God's work in our lives, but I quote them to bring the great grace and great power He provides us through the Spirit to your attention. There is no reason for sin in a believer's life. "You, dear children, are from God and have overcome them, because the one who is in you is greater than the one who is in the world" (1 John 4:4).

CHAPTER 8

OBEDIENCE AND FAITH

*Now faith is being sure of what we hope for
and certain of what we do not see. (Heb. 11:1)*

The word "obedience" has a poor reputation today,
even in the Church. For many of us, our obedience has
been poor all our lives (whether towards our parents, our
supervisors, or in the military) because we did not want
to do the things we were told to do. When your father
told you to do something, you probably did not say, "Yes-
sir, Dad, I'd love to clean the basement every day, just to
please you, I love you so much."

Christians have also come to associate obedience with
works-righteousness. We know from the Scripture that
works-righteousness is wrong—that the grace of God saves

us—and we have put obedience into the "works" category, so telling people to obey is not acceptable. What is the result? Christians who are "faith" people, but who are not obedient people. This is a major reason that there is so much disobedience in the Christian church today.

Yet the Bible uses the word "obey" in many places. So we must find out the biblical view of obedience. My thesis is that *obedience is closely related to faith and is **not related to works at all***.

What is faith? Faith is love upwards. It is our way of expressing love to God. Faith is also obedience. Look at the beginning of Romans, one of the great books on salvation by faith:

> Through him and for his name's sake we received grace and apostleship to call people from among all the Gentiles to *the obedience that comes from faith*. (Rom. 1:5)

This verse speaks of obedience and faith together. Now look at the way Romans ends:

> Now to him who is able to establish you by my gospel and the proclamation of Jesus Christ, according to the revelation of the mystery hidden for long ages past, but now revealed and made known through the prophetic writings by the command of the eternal God, so *that all nations might believe and obey him*— to the only wise God be glory forever through Jesus Christ! Amen. (Rom. 16:25–27)

Romans makes a strong connection between faith and obedience. It starts out with "the *obedience* that comes from *faith*" and ends with "*believe* and *obey* Him."

Hebrews 11 is the great faith chapter of the New Testament. Some of the expressions in it might surprise you. Look first at how Hebrews defines faith:

> Now faith is being sure of what we hope for and certain of what we do not see. (Heb. 11:1)

Faith requires ignorance. Now look at verses 6–7:

> And without faith it is impossible to please God, because anyone who comes to him must believe that he exists and that he rewards those who earnestly seek him. *By faith, Noah*, when warned about things not yet seen, in holy fear *built an ark* to save his family. (Heb. 11:6–7)

Hebrews tells us that Noah built the ark in holy fear. But did he also obey when he built the ark? Yes. God had told him to do it. He told Noah to build a ship, and Noah built it. By faith, he obeyed.

Question: Would Noah have been saved if he had not built the ark? *No.* Suppose he had said, "God, You know I don't believe in works-righteousness. I believe in salvation by faith, and I believe You are going to send a flood—but if You think I'm going to build a ship in this desert, You're crazy. Think what the neighbors would say." Faith required that Noah build. Noah's faith and Noah's obedience were the same thing. If he had not been obedient by building the ark, he would not have had faith, and he would not have been saved.

Godly faith is not an abstract concept. It is an active service. There is no way Noah could have had genuine faith without building that ark. Simply saying he had faith did not mean he had it. Such "faith" is not faith at all. Faith requires obedience. Faith required that Noah *obey* God's command to build a ship in the desert.

James 2:14 says that faith without works is dead. James was speaking of works of obedience, not works-righteousness. Works cannot save you in the least, but genuine, saving faith produces works of obedience. Works are the natural fruit of living faith. James was not trying to establish who had works, but who had *faith*. "You show me your faith without your works; I will show you my faith by my works." Does this person's faith obey, or does his faith just talk, James asks. Faith that just talks, he says, is not faith at all. Real faith takes action.

The following is part of a letter I received: "I realize that we are justified by faith. Paul says this very clearly [in Romans]. But James says in James 2:24 NIV that we are justified by works. I realize that we are justified by faith and the work of the Spirit leads us to works to demonstrate our faith and serve the Lord, but James seems to clearly contradict Paul's teaching. Can you by any chance reconcile this apparent contradiction for me?"

James and Paul do not contradict each other. We are justified by grace through faith alone. Remember that Paul uses Abraham as an example of justification by faith in Romans 4:2–3: "If, in fact, Abraham was justified by works, he had something to boast about—but not before God. What does the Scripture say? 'Abraham believed God, and it was credited to him as righteousness.'"

Paul is quoting Genesis 15:4–6 where Abram had arrived in the land of Canaan when he was seventy-five years old and Sarai was sixty-five.

Hebrews 11 also uses Abraham as an example of faith: "By faith Abraham, when called to go to a place he would later receive as his inheritance, obeyed and went, even though he did not know where he was going" (Heb. 11:8). By faith Abraham obeyed and went to make his home in Canaan.

But James also uses Abraham as an example:

> You foolish man, do you want evidence that faith without deeds is useless? Was not our ancestor Abraham considered righteous for what he did when he offered his son Isaac on the altar? You see that his faith and his actions were working together, and *his faith was made complete by what he did.* And the scripture was fulfilled that says, *"Abraham believed God, and it was credited to him as righteousness,"* and he was called God's friend. You see that a person is justified by what he does and not by faith alone. (James 2:20–24)

The quotation, "Abraham believed God and it was credited to him as righteousness" refers first to the promise given when Abraham was seventy-five and moved to Canaan, second to the birth of Isaac when Abraham was a hundred years old, and finally to the sacrifice of Isaac.

Abraham's faith was a response to the faithfulness of God. His trust was in God, not in his own faith or his own obedience. His faith was expressed in action, not in words only. Abraham could not have had faith without the obedience of leaving his people and his land at God's command. He could not have had faith without sacrificing his son. That faith would have been dead. But he believed God's word that "it is through Isaac that your offspring will be reckoned" (Gen. 21:12), so he obeyed.

Yes, James says in 2:24 that we are justified by works. The key verse, though, is verse 18: "Show me your faith without deeds and *I will show you my faith by what I do*." Who has faith? The one who *says* he has it, or the one who *shows* he has it? Of course, you can do "good works" without faith. That saves no one, "because by observing the law no one will be justified" (Gal. 2:16). But you cannot have real, believing faith without works, because faith in God naturally results in obedience. The works establish whose faith is real. "As the body without the spirit is dead, so faith without deeds is dead" (James 2:26).

Biblical faith is not just a feeling. It is agreeing with God and taking action on what He tells you to do—in obedience. Suppose you are a translator working on putting the Scriptures into a primitive language that has only 800 words in its vocabulary, and no abstract words. What are you going to do when you get to John 3:16? How are you going to translate "believe"? Translators often render it "obey," because that word is usually in the vocabulary when "belief" and "faith" are not. When they do this, they are very close to the meaning.

There is no such connection between works-righteousness and obedience. Most works-righteousness is really obeying yourself: you get to choose what you are going to do to please God. But God did not give us the Ten Options—He gave us the Ten Commandments. The New Testament is also filled with commands. We are to respond to them in faithful, glad obedience.

"Yes," you say, "but these passages are not talking about being converted. Is obedience also involved in saving faith?" That is a good question. Since salvation is by faith and obedience and faith are so closely tied together, it makes sense that obedience should also be closely related to salvation.

> Although he was a son, he learned obedience from
> what he suffered and, once made perfect, he became
> *the source of eternal salvation for all who obey him.*
> (Heb. 5:8–9)

That is a salvation verse. Have you ever heard it preached by evangelists? Probably not. When people give the gospel, they usually stick to passages like Ephesians 2:8–9, John 1:12, and Titus 3:5. Evangelists won't touch verses like Hebrews 5:8 with a forty-foot pole because they know that people will make the mistake of thinking they are preaching salvation by works. Yet Christ became the source of eternal salvation for all who obey Him. This only sounds like a contradiction if you think that obedience is different from faith.

> Since it is a righteous thing with God to repay with
> tribulation those who trouble you, and to give you
> who are troubled rest with us when the Lord Jesus
> is revealed from heaven with His mighty angels, in

> flaming fire taking vengeance on those who do not
> know God, and on those who do not *obey the gospel*
> of our Lord Jesus Christ. (2 Thess. 1:6–8 NKJV)

This is another salvation verse with the word "obedience" in it. The gospel has to be *obeyed* in order to save. This is stronger than simple believe-ism, stronger than just signing a card. I am not saying people cannot be saved by going forward at a gospel meeting and signing a card, but I believe we have truncated the gospel and the proper response to it by a hollowed-out definition of belief. Remember again what James says: "Thus also, faith by itself, if it does not have works, is dead" (James 2:17 NKJV). Real faith results in action. The act of signing a card or saying you believe by itself will not save you. That is why some "saved" people are not saved. Many "born-again" people have not been born again. Obedience does not just come after conversion. The gospel itself needs to be obeyed.

How do you obey the gospel? Look at Acts 17. In this chapter, Paul walked into Athens and found the city wholly given to idolatry. The Athenians were very religious people. They had altars to all the gods. They even had an altar to the unknown God, in case they had forgotten one. Rather than stopping to marvel at the Parthenon and the other wonders of the city, Paul saw this altar and immediately began to preach to the Athenians: "The God you do not know, I will declare to you. He is the God who made everything."

> Therefore, since we are God's offspring, we should
> not think that the divine being is like gold or silver or

stone—an image made by man's design and skill. In
the past God overlooked such ignorance, but now *he
commands all people everywhere to repent.* For he has
set a day when he will judge the world with justice by
the man he has appointed. He has given proof of this to
all men by raising him from the dead. (Acts 17:29–31)

Since God has commanded all people everywhere to
repent, the very beginning of your life in Christ was a response to a command. *By repenting you obey the gospel.*
Whom does the command to repent include? *Everyone.*
From now on, Paul says, there are no exceptions for anyone
anywhere concerning repentance.

When you became a Christian, did you repent? Yes.
What were you doing when you repented? You were *obeying a command.* You say, "I didn't know it was a command.
I thought I believed by faith and received grace." You did—
but you were told to do it. When you turned to God the Father through Jesus Christ, you were obeying the command
of the gospel. You also obey the gospel by *believing.* That
belief has two aspects: one, agreeing that the Word of God
is true, and the other, being willing to trust it, to act on it.

Therefore, when we present the gospel, speaking on behalf of Jesus Christ, we can command people to repent.
Their response to this command is obedience by *faith.*
Their repentance is efficacious because of the work of Jesus Christ.

CHAPTER 9

OBEDIENCE AND LOVE

If you obey my commands, you will remain in my love,
just as I have obeyed my Father's commands
and remain in his love. (John 15:10)

Obedience and love are also closely connected, just like obedience and faith. The greatest command in Scripture is "Love the Lord your God." "Jesus replied: 'Love the Lord your God with all your heart and with all your soul and with all your mind.' This is the first and greatest commandment" (Matt. 22:37–38). Love is obedience to the greatest command. Jesus also commands us to love each other:

> A new command I give you: Love one another. As I have loved you, so you must love one another. By this

> all men will know that you are my disciples, if you
> love one another. (John 13:34–35)

> And he has given us this command: Whoever loves
> God must also love his brother. (1 John 4:21)

How do we express love? It is not by *saying* that we love. There are two main expressions of love. Love *downwards* is sacrificial: "For God so loved the world that He gave His only-begotten Son" (John 3:16 NKJV). Love *upwards* is obedience. Jesus said, "If you love Me, keep My commands" (John 14:15 NKJV). Fathers sacrifice for their children because they love them; but children do not say, "Dad, if you love me, keep my commands." Children show *their* love by obeying.

> "*Whoever has my commands and obeys them, he is the one who loves me.* He who loves me will be loved by my Father, and I too will love him and show myself to him." Then Judas (not Judas Iscariot) said, "But, Lord, why do you intend to show yourself to us and not to the world?" Jesus replied, "*If anyone loves me, he will obey my teaching.* My Father will love him, and we will come to him and make our home with him. *He who does not love me will not obey my teaching.* These words you hear are not my own; they belong to the Father who sent me." (John 14:21–24)

We show love for Jesus by obeying Him. All true obedience is done out of love for the One who loved us and gave His life for us.

CHAPTER 10

OBEDIENCE
AND PRAYER

*I want men everywhere to lift up holy hands in
prayer, without anger or disputing. (1 Tim. 2:8)*

Salvation is by faith through grace. Obedience is by faith
too, which means we also obey by grace (see Galatians
3). One of the implications of this is that the *quality* of our
obedience is inextricably linked with the closeness of our
walk with God. A major component of that walk is prayer.

> And pray in the Spirit on all occasions, with all
> kinds of prayers and requests. With this in mind, be
> alert and always keep on praying for all the saints.
> (Eph. 6:18)

"Pray...on all occasions." This means praying all the time, for whatever reason. You do not have to be in a special posture or a special place to pray. In Matthew 6, when Jesus said to enter into your closet to pray, He said that to keep people from praying in a public, ostentatious way like the Pharisees did. God hears you in secret, but when you are praying you can be in secret anywhere.

"Pray...with all kinds of prayers and requests." What can you pray about? Anything. *Everything.* You can take anything to the Lord in prayer, no matter how big or how insignificant. There is nothing that is not worth taking to God. You will not be wasting His time.

"Pray in the Spirit." Praying in the Spirit means that the Holy Spirit is authoring your prayer or helping you in prayer. Sometimes people tie this passage to Romans 8:26, which says, "In the same way, the Spirit helps us in our weakness. We do not know what we ought to pray, but the Spirit himself intercedes for us with *groans that words cannot express.*" The King James says, "groanings that cannot be uttered." Words cannot express this prayer. This is not the same as praying in tongues, because tongues are words, utterances. This is praying from the depths of your heart with the Holy Spirit praying for you according to the will of God.[8] The context of the prayer in Romans 8:18–27 is praying for the second coming of Jesus. The whole creation groans (as in childbirth). We groan inwardly. The Holy Spirit groans. Other Holy Spirit-authored prayers

8 This is not a comment that you should not pray in tongues. I am just saying that these two verses are not speaking about that.

with words can be found in Philippians 1:9–11, Colossians 1:9–12, and Ephesians 1:16–19 and 3:14–21.

"Be alert and always keep on praying for all the saints." Have you ever fallen asleep praying? When I was a freshman at the Naval Academy, Carryl Whipple, one of my classmates, invited me to attend an early morning Bible study-prayer meeting that met seven days a week. I was not a Christian, and I did not want to go, but I also did not want to tell the fellow who invited me that I didn't want to go. The meeting was at 5:45 a.m. Reveille was not until 6:15. So I told Carryl that I would love to go, but I did not wake up at that time, and my roommate would kill me if an alarm clock went off. He said, "I'll wake you up." I did not know how to get out of it. That was my first step towards becoming a Christian. (I received Christ the following fall.)

I went to the study for the next three years. By my senior year, I was a mature Christian in relation to everyone else in the study. At the Naval Academy, if you are a senior, you have the stripes and the authority, so I was in charge of the studies, and I was responsible for waking everyone else up. Sometimes I would not get up, and people would come to me during the day and say, "How come you didn't wake me up? I've had a rough day missing that prayer meeting."

I would say, "Don't worry; so did I. It won't happen again." And the next morning I would sleep in again.

Finally I went to my friend Eric Nelson, who was running a study in one of the other wings. I said, "Eric, do you ever have this problem?"

"Yeah. I just ask the Lord the night before to wake me up at 5:30."

"Really?"

"Yeah, really."

So that night I asked the Lord to wake me up at 5:30, and I woke up at 5:30 right on the nose. I thought, "Boy, this is great." I did that for several days, and I always woke up when I had asked the Lord to wake me up.

Then, one day, having asked the Lord, I woke up at 5:30 and thought, "Oh well, I can pray just as easily here in bed as I can at the prayer meeting." So I said a little conscience-easer prayer, rolled over, and went back to sleep.

After a few complaints on that one, I went to Eric again. "Eric, you're right—I wake up at 5:30 when I ask God to wake me up, but I roll over and go back to sleep."

He said, "I had the same problem. So I memorized Luke 22:46 where Jesus is speaking to His disciples in the garden and says, 'Why sleep ye? Rise and pray lest ye enter into temptation.'"

So I memorized that verse, prayed the night before, woke up at 5:30, started to fall asleep again, and the verse hit me. I could not get away with sleeping in after that. *Rise and pray.* It became a real victory. In fact, it became such a victory that I woke up singing for the rest of my senior year.

In the spring, I graduated from the Academy and went home on leave, then was stationed in the Far East in the Korean War. I had night-watches on the ship. One time, a sailor woke me up for my watch at 3:30 a.m. As I woke up, I was singing, and I know that sailor thought there was something wrong with me. Wonderful things happen with prayer.

"Pray also for me, that whenever I open my mouth, words may be given me so I will fearlessly make known the mystery of the gospel, for which I am an ambassador in chains. Pray that I may declare it fearlessly, as I should" (Eph. 6:19–20). Fear is one of the main problems Christians have with sharing the gospel. To overcome it, they crank up their courage and go knock on doors. But that is not how we are meant to get our courage. We get it by having friends pray for us. If you are reminded to pray for me, pray this, that whenever I open my mouth, I will make known the mystery of the gospel without fear.

Paul requests this same prayer in other places in the New Testament. "Devote yourselves to prayer, being watchful and thankful. And pray for us too, that God may open a door for our message, so that we may proclaim the mystery of Christ, for which I am in chains. Pray that I may proclaim it clearly, as I should" (Col. 4:2–4).

Pray for your fellow Christians the way Paul prayed for the believers in Colossae: "For this reason, since the day we heard about you, we have not stopped praying for you and asking God to fill you with the knowledge of his will through all spiritual wisdom and understanding" (Col. 1:9)."

Christians often ask me how to know the will of God. One way is to have your friends pray that you will be filled with the knowledge of His will with all spiritual wisdom and understanding. Paul prays this for the believers "in order that you may live a life worthy of the Lord" (Col. 1:10a).

Much Christian teaching today is on being forgiven for your unworthiness, but Paul prayed that the Colossians would live a life worthy of the Lord by *doing it right the first time.* We know that they will, because it was an inspired prayer.

Worthy of the Lord is a lot to ask for, isn't it? Yes, it is. But what else would we pray? "Lord, please fill these believers half-full with the knowledge of Your will. We would like them to be partly worthy of You." That's silly! Pray big, and go into specifics. That is how the Apostle Paul prayed. We are content to pray, "Lord, bless Uncle Joe." We do not pray that Uncle Joe would be "filled with the knowledge of His will through all spirtual wisdom and understanding." We should.

Occasionally there is someone in a congregation who seems to be filled with the knowledge of God's will. It drives the rest of the congregation crazy. People do not like it when others are godlier than they are. So in many ways, we are keeping each other down. We do not want others to be filled all the way. If all my congregation were, I would not have to show up on Sunday morning.

"And we pray this in order that you may live a life worthy of the Lord and may please him in every way: bearing fruit in every good work, growing in the knowledge of God, being strengthened with all power according to his glorious might, so that you may have great endurance and patience" (Col. 1:10–11). Paul is not praying for little things here. I encourage you to pray for each other this way. The Colossians could not suddenly live a life worthy of the Lord on their own. They had to have God's help in it, and God's help comes because people *pray*. Pray for one another that God would provide help to His people for living a life of obedience and trust. It takes the sweat and the trying out of obedience.

CHAPTER 11

GOD'S COMMANDS

*But just as he who called you is holy,
so be holy in all you do. (1 Pet. 1:15)*

The deity, death, and resurrection of Jesus Christ are the motivation, the power, and the provision for everything in our lives. Consequently, the discussion of almost any spiritual subject should point to the gospel sooner or later.

"Paul, a servant of Christ Jesus, called to be an apostle and set apart for the gospel of God—the gospel he promised beforehand through his prophets in the Holy Scriptures regarding his Son...who through the Spirit of holiness was *declared with power to be the Son of God by his resurrection* from the dead: Jesus Christ our Lord" (Rom.

1:1–4). The resurrection of Jesus Christ declares with power that Jesus is the Son of God and that He is Lord.

Let's return again to Romans. "Jesus Christ our Lord. Through him and for his name's sake, we received grace and apostleship to call people from among all the Gentiles to *the obedience that comes from faith*. And you also are among those who are called to belong to Jesus Christ" (Rom. 1:4b-6). This is a very strong passage. Through Jesus Christ our Lord, we received grace, and we received orders. We have been sent—to bring about what? "The obedience that comes from faith" for the sake of His name among all the nations.

Obedience depends very much on recognizing the authority of the person giving the orders. Someone who is known to have great power gets obedience more easily. For instance, as a child, were you more quickly obedient to your mother or to your father? Your mother could make loud noises. She could scream and holler and yell without results. But your father could give the order in a low tone, and you would jump to it. Sometimes my father wouldn't even have to *say* anything.

The character and quality of our obedience to God reflects our view of who He is. When I was in Navy boot camp, the only person I saw at first was the chief petty officer. After a while, I ran into ensigns and lieutenants junior-grade. They did not look that powerful, but I knew they were officers, so I did what they said. Then one time at Camp Peary, Virginia, I gave one of the lieutenants a lot of lip. It showed that my view of his power and authority was not great, even though I was only a seaman. Unfortunately for me, he had real authority, and he made me wish I had not given him the lip—but nevertheless, my *view* of his authority was low, and I had *acted* accordingly.

Then I entered the Naval Academy. The very first day, I went through the line and collected my uniforms. Then I went up to my room. My roommate had not arrived, so I was alone. I got out of my sailor's uniform to put on my new midshipman's uniform. In between getting out of the one and getting into the other, I was in that state called buck naked when a commander walked into the room in his service-dress whites, gleaming like the angel Gabriel, with his dress sword hanging by his side. I did not know whether to stand at attention or jump out the window. He could have told me to do pretty much anything, and I would have done it in a hurry.

We ought to be in even more of a hurry to obey Jesus. This goes right back to the gospel. Jesus Christ is what? Lord and God. He is "declared to be the Son of God, with power."

There is a strong connection between the lordship of Christ, the gospel, and our obedience:

> For none of us lives to himself, and no one dies to himself. For if we live, we *live to the Lord*; and *if we die, we die to the Lord*. Therefore, whether we live or die, we are the Lord's. For *to this end Christ died and rose and lived again, that He might be Lord* of both the dead and the living. (Rom. 14:7–9 NKJV)

> For Christ's love compels us, because we are convinced that one died for all, and therefore all died.

> And he died for all, that those who live should no
> longer live for themselves but for him who died for
> them and was raised again. (2 Cor. 5:14)

There is the gospel. Jesus died and rose again so that we might live for Him. What is the significance of Christ's death? If He died for all, then all *have died*. But things did not stop there. If we died with Him, we also rose with Him. We experienced both a spiritual death and a spiritual resurrection. When we identify our lives with the gospel, we *die to sin and rise to life*. To what end? That we might live for Him. Are you going to obey the One who died and rose again, or are you going to obey yourself? Obedience is the proper result of the gospel; you cannot separate the two.

In the early 20th century, a missionary named C.T. Studd founded a group called the Worldwide Evangelization Crusade. He made a statement that is quoted often in that mission, and that is this: "If Jesus Christ be God and died for me, then there is no sacrifice too great for me to make for Him." When you read verses on the lordship of Jesus Christ (these occur every few sentences throughout the New Testament) pay attention to them; His lordship is the foundation of our walk with Him. In Matthew 28, Jesus said, "All authority in heaven and on earth has been given to Me. Therefore go and make disciples of all nations." When He says "Go," we do it because of who told us to—the One who has absolute authority.

The second component of obedience is *knowing what the orders are*. You can have great respect for the boss, but you cannot obey unless you know what he is telling you to do.

Our orders are primarily found in the Bible. Occasionally I used to hear people say, "God told me to do this." Now I hear it fairly often. Frequently when people say that God has told them to do something, that something is extrabiblical. They claim that God has communicated revelation to them, and then they go do whatever the revelation was. If these same Christians were as quickly obedient to the commands in Scripture as they are to the things that "God told them" to do, the world would be a much godlier place.

I am not saying that God does not tell people to do things, but often this sort of "revelation" is nothing more than an excuse people make to justify doing what they already wanted to do. It works this way: when someone tells me that God told him to do something, what can I say? Nothing except that he had better go do it, in case God actually *did* tell him to. It cuts out any possibility of discussion. I cannot reason with him—though I do wonder why he is coming to me for counsel if he has orders straight from the Lord Himself.

You must know your orders, and the primary place to get them is the Bible. There are the Ten Commandments and many, many commands in the New Testament as well. A few of these were given just to a particular person, but most of them apply to all of us.

The commands we are given as Christians and the law that was given in the Old Testament have different purposes. The purpose of the law was to bring sin to people's attention. When a person knows the law and is aware that he has not obeyed it, he realizes that he needs grace. After we have received grace, the commands are no longer merely measuring sticks of right and wrong; now we are expected to actually obey them. This obedience is possible because God has given us the provision through grace.

God did not throw out the Old Testament law when the New Testament was written. His concept of morality has not changed. The law merely has a different *function* for someone who is under grace than for someone who is still outside Christianity. It condemns those outside, and because of that it is their guide to Christ.

> But the Scripture has confined all under sin, that the promise by faith in Jesus Christ might be given to those who believe. But before faith came, we were kept under guard by the law, kept for the faith which would afterward be revealed. Therefore *the law was our tutor to bring us to Christ*, that we might be justified by faith. But after faith has come, we are no longer under a tutor. (Gal. 3:22–25 NKJV)

The law brings us to Christ for salvation by making us realize our sinfulness.

The New Testament does not change the Old Testament law—it clarifies it. The commands in the New Testament point to the *motives* behind our actions, the heart condition. Look at Matthew 5:

> You have heard that it was said to the people long ago, "Do not murder, and anyone who murders will be subject to judgment." But I tell you that anyone who is angry with his brother will be subject to

judgment. Again, anyone who says to his brother, "Raca," is answerable to the Sanhedrin. But anyone who says, "You fool!" will be in danger of the fire of hell...You have heard that it was said, "Do not commit adultery." But I tell you that anyone who looks at a woman lustfully has already committed adultery with her in his heart. (Matt. 5:21–22, 27–28)

Now that you are under grace, it is realistically possible to not commit murder. However, God also expects you to not even *think* it: you will not lose your temper, you will not hate your brother, and you will not call him a fool. This goes much deeper than the simple commands of the Old Testament.

One clarification: before Jesus' time, God *did* expect His children to have pure hearts. Commands that go as far as the heart motives were not necessary for pointing people to God's grace, since the prohibition of the actions themselves (e.g., murder, lying, or adultery) condemned 100 percent of the people. Why "super-condemn" them by expounding on the motives of the heart as well? God has always expected the people who know Him to live godly lives (cf. Leviticus 19:2, 18). He does not have to wheel out the "super-expression" of the commands to get those who do not know Him to realize their need for grace.

Know the commands. Do not be ignorant of them, and do not take them with a grain of salt. Love the Lord your God with everything you are, and love your neighbor as yourself. But after that, *get into the details*.

First, do this: "Get rid of all bitterness, rage and anger, brawling and slander, along with every form of malice"

(Eph. 4:31). Then this: "Be kind and compassionate to one another, forgiving each other, just as in Christ God forgave you" (Eph. 4:32).

The sins in the first list need to disappear from your life. Bitterness is a heart attitude. Tender-heartedness is also a heart attitude. Can you be bitter and tender-hearted at the same time? No. One of them has to go. Get rid of *all bitterness*.[9] Holiness has no chance if righteousness is not maintained.

As you read the New Testament, you will come across commands like this one: "And we exhort you, brethren, admonish the idlers, encourage the faint-hearted, help the weak, be patient with them all" (1 Thess. 5:14 RSV).You have the authority to admonish the weak. But God says, "Be patient with them all," so you cannot admonish them impatiently. You are commanded to chew a man out for being lazy, but you are not allowed to do it with any kind of irritation.

"See that none of you repays evil for evil, but always seek to do good to one another and to all. Rejoice always" (1 Thess. 5:15–16 RSV). Is that a suggestion? No.

"Pray constantly" (1 Thess. 5:17 RSV). Is that good advice? No. It is a command.

> Give thanks in all circumstances, for this is the will of God in Christ Jesus for you. (1 Thess. 5:18 RSV)

> But test everything. Hold fast what is good. Abstain from every form of evil. (1 Thess. 5:21–22 RSV)

9 See *How to be Free from Bitterness* by Jim Wilson, available at ccmbooks.org.

None of the commands in the New Testament are moderate ones. Paul never says to take it easy. Do not equivocate on them. Get in the habit of looking at every command plainly, with *no purpose of evasion*.[10] Do not say, "Yes, sir," and put off the obedience hoping that God will overlook it. Do not say, "Yes, I will obey," when in your heart you have no intention of obeying. If you look at the Scripture frankly, searching out who Christ is and what He tells us to be and to do, your first reaction should be something like, "Woe is me, for I am undone! I have not even known who He is, and I certainly have not been paying attention to what He says. I have been riding on being saved by grace and going to heaven in the future, and the concept of present obedience to an almighty Lord has not even entered my head."

The beginning of every act of obedience is recognizing that you are not obedient. Imagine you are in the Navy, and your commanding officer tells you go jump across the Chesapeake Bay. You could take several views of that.

"Who does he think he is? I don't have to do what he says. I'm not going to jump over the Chesapeake Bay." You intend to disobey, and you know that you are disobeying.

"Well, he's my boss, and he said to jump over the bay, but he knows I can't jump over it, so he must have meant jump *in* it." So you go running off to the bay, jump in, come back soaking wet, and say, "I've carried out your orders."

---

10 "Purpose of evasion" is a phrase from the oath of citizenship or the oath commissioned officers take in the armed forces of the United States: "I take this obligation freely without any mental reservation or purpose of evasion, so help me God."

He says, "It looks like you fell short."

This is what Christians tend to do with the Bible. They take a command that sounds impossible (and they all sound impossible) and say, "God knows I can't pray constantly; therefore, he must have meant pray once in a while. I'll do that." That is not obeying.

"He's the boss, and he said to jump over the bay. I can't jump over the bay; maybe I had better ask him for help. Or maybe I should go take jumping lessons." Here there is recognition of what the boss actually said, that the boss *is* the boss, and that you are not going to change the command. You are willing to learn how to jump over the bay.

However, our obedience to God is not impossible in the same way as jumping over the bay, because God always provides the means for obeying His "impossible" commands.

Be careful that you do not bring God's commands down to size. "Rejoice always." Do you rejoice in the circumstances, or do you rejoice because of the circumstances? Habakkuk 3:17–18 describes a farmer who had a bad year (and that's putting it mildly): "Though the fig tree does not bud and there are *no grapes* on the vines, though *the olive crop fails* and the fields produce *no food*, though there are *no sheep* in the pen and *no cattle* in the stalls, *yet I will rejoice in the* Lord, I will be joyful in God my Savior."

The Lord is where the joy is. We can obey the command to rejoice always because we do not rejoice in the circumstances. True joy is in *the Lord in the circumstances*. We always have Him. In a bad situation, we rejoice in the God of our salvation. He is always true.

Habakkuk described a bad situation. Luke 10 describes the opposite. Jesus had sent seventy out, two by two: "The seventy returned with joy, saying, 'Lord, even the demons are subject to us in your name.' And he said to them, 'I saw Satan fall like lightning from heaven; behold, I have given you authority to tread upon serpents and scorpions and over all the power of the enemy, and nothing shall hurt you. Nevertheless, *do not rejoice in this, but rejoice that your names are written in heaven*'" (Luke 10:17–20 RSV).

Here are two cases, one where the circumstances were bad, and one where the circumstances were good. In both instances, God tells us not to rejoice in the circumstances, but to rejoice *in Him* and in our salvation.

CHAPTER 12

TRYING TO OBEY

*And by that will, we have been made holy
through the sacrifice of the body of Jesus Christ
once for all. (Heb. 10:10)*

The world is made up of two types of people: those who
want to earn their way to heaven and those who do
not. The first group follows what is called natural theology.
It sets up standards that it thinks are God's and then tries
to achieve them. Each religion does it differently—Hindus
one way, Buddhists another—but if you get to heaven, it
is in some measure through your own effort, whether by
making your pilgrimage to Mecca, fasting during Rama-
dan, not playing cards, or going to church every Sunday.

Within Christian circles, we are schizophrenic. We *teach* salvation by faith—but we *live* natural theology. Protestants and Catholics both teach that we come to know God through repentance and belief in the deity, death, burial, and resurrection of Jesus Christ. At the same time, however, they assume a set of standards we must meet in order to make it to heaven. These cannot both be true, "for if righteousness could be gained through the law, Christ died for nothing" (Gal. 2:21). You cannot have the effort of achieving the standard and the "no effort" of grace through faith at the same time. *Either salvation is a free gift, or it is not a free gift.* If you have to earn it *even one tiny bit*, it is not free.

> When Christ came as high priest of the good things that are already here, he went through the greater and more perfect tabernacle that is not man-made, that is to say, not a part of this creation. He did not enter by means of the blood of goats and calves; but he entered the most holy place once for all by his own blood, having obtained eternal redemption. The blood of goats and bulls and the ashes of a heifer sprinkled on those who are ceremonially unclean sanctify them so they are outwardly clean. How much more, then, will the blood of Christ, who through the eternal Spirit offered himself unblemished to God, cleanse our consciences from acts that lead to death, so that we may serve the living God! (Heb. 9:11–14)

Through His death, Christ cleansed our conscience. That is the only way it can get clean. And when it is cleansed, it is cleansed once for all.

Nor did he enter heaven to offer himself again and
again, the way the high priest enters the Most Holy
Place every year with blood that is not his own. Then
Christ would have had to suffer many times since the
creation of the world. But now he has appeared once
for all at the end of the ages *to do away with sin by
the sacrifice of himself.* Just as man is destined to die
once, and after that to face judgment, so Christ was
sacrificed once to take away the sins of many people;
and he will appear a second time, not to bear sin, but
to bring salvation to those who are waiting for him.
(Heb. 9:25–28)

Jesus Christ did *everything* for our salvation. There is not
one bit that man can do. Jesus paid for all of it, for all time.

And by that will, we have been made holy through
the sacrifice of the body of Jesus Christ once for all...
But when this priest had offered for all time one sacrifice for sins, he sat down at the right hand of God.
Since that time he waits for his enemies to be made
his footstool, because by one sacrifice he has made
perfect forever those who are being made holy. (Heb.
10:10, 12–14)

Jesus Christ took care of all our sins, makes us holy, and
takes us to heaven.

Therefore, brothers, since we have confidence to enter the Most Holy Place by the blood of Jesus, by a
new and living way opened for us through the cur-
tain, that is, his body, and since we have a great
priest over the house of God, *let us draw near to God*

> *with a sincere heart in full assurance of faith, hav-*
> *ing our hearts sprinkled to cleanse us from a guilty*
> *conscience* and having our bodies washed with pure
> water. *Let us hold unswervingly to the hope we profess,*
> *for he who promised is faithful.* And let us consider
> how we may spur one another on toward love and
> good deeds. Let us not give up meeting together, as
> some are in the habit of doing, but let us encourage
> one another—and all the more as you see the Day
> approaching. (Heb. 10:19–25)

If you have been relying on the death of Jesus Christ for
your sins but at the same time trying to live worthy of being
a Christian, you will probably find that you still have a guilty
conscience. Realize that Jesus Christ did it all, receive Him
with thanksgiving, and your conscience will be cleansed—
and not by any self-effort. *He will cleanse it for you.*

The prerequisite for being a Christian is to be bad. You
cannot go to heaven if you are good. All other world religions teach that you have to be good to go to heaven, and
many Christians teach it, too. The Bible says you must
be bad to be saved. Jesus Christ did not come to heal the
healthy, but the sick. He came to save the *sinners*.

> And when the scribes and Pharisees saw Him eating
> with the tax collectors and sinners, they said to His
> disciples, "How is it that He eats and drinks with tax
> collectors and sinners?" When Jesus heard it, He said to
> them, "Those who are well have no need of a physician,
> but those who are sick. I did not come to call the righ-
> teous, but sinners, to repentance." (Mark 2:16–17 NKJV)

You have to be a sinner to be saved. If you think you are
not a sinner, Jesus Christ cannot help you. But if you know
you are a sinner and your conscience is unclean, then come
to Him. If you try to clean it yourself, it will stay dirty.

Just as our salvation was through the work of Jesus
Christ alone, so is our Christian walk.

> So then, just as you received Christ Jesus as Lord,
> continue to live in him, rooted and built up in him,
> strengthened in the faith as you were taught and
> overflowing with thankfulness. (Col. 2:6–7)

The Navigators have a Bible study called 2:7. It is taken
from Colossians 2:7, which starts in the middle of a sentence—"rooted and built up in Him, strengthened in the
faith as you were taught and overflowing with thankful-
ness." But the key part of the passage is in verse 6: "Just as
you received Christ Jesus as Lord, continue to live in Him."
How did you receive Christ Jesus as Lord? By effort? By trying to? No. It was by God's grace giving and faith receiving.
There was zero effort on your part. Scripture says so.

I want to make this very clear. We receive Christ Jesus
as Lord by grace through faith, plus nothing. No effort. In
fact, when we receive Christ, we *quit* trying. You cannot try
and trust at the same time. It is impossible. If you try and
trust, what you are really doing is just not trusting. Do you
know the hymn, "Try to Obey"? No. We sing, "Trust and
obey," but then we go out and *try*. The person who tries
to obey God is guaranteed to fall, because sooner or later
he is going to run out of gas. And the devil will be there

waiting for him when he runs dry. The tryer runs out; the truster does not.

Live by grace. The entire book of Galatians was written on this subject. The third chapter starts out, "You foolish Galatians" (Gal. 3:1a). In some translations it says, "idiots" for "foolish." "You *foolish* Galatians! Who has bewitched you? Before your very eyes Jesus Christ was clearly portrayed as crucified" (Gal. 3:1). This is the same language Paul uses in Romans 6. Christ died to sin once for all, and we died to sin with Him.

"I would like to learn just one thing from you: Did you receive the Spirit by observing the law or by believing what you heard?" (Gal. 3:2). The answer is "by believing." But Paul does not wait for the answer. He knows that the Galatians already know this.

"Did you receive the Spirit by observing the law or by believing what you heard? Are you so foolish? After beginning with the Spirit, are you now trying to attain your goal by human effort? Have you suffered so much for nothing, if it really was for nothing? Does God give you his Spirit and work miracles among you because you observe the law, or because you believe what you heard?" (Gal. 3:2b-5). The Galatians entered the kingdom by belief, and now they have regressed into trying. That is idiotic, Paul says.

The law has no power to make us obey. What the law could not do, God did for us through the Cross: "For *what the law was powerless to do* in that it was weakened by the sinful nature, *God did* by sending his own Son in the likeness of sinful man to be a sin offering. And so he condemned sin in sinful man, in order that the righteous requirements of the law might be fully met in us" (Rom. 8:3–4a).

We can obey the Ten Commandments because of the Cross, but we do not obey them by trying. The standard is the same, but we live it out by the power of God. Are you a try-er or a doer? Confess it as sin and say, "I am not going to try; I am going to trust and obey. I entered the kingdom by trusting God; I will walk by trusting Him."

Man has always been reckoned righteous by faith. The law never justified anyone. It was never intended to justify anyone. Salvation has always been through Christ. His death was prefigured in the sacrifices of the Old Testament, but it transcends history. He died for everyone who lived before, and He died for everyone who has lived since.

The sacrifices in the Old Testament were like communion is today. We look back to the death of Christ; they looked forward to it. The animal sacrifices were never meant to be a means of forgiveness. They could not save. They were there to point the way to the one sacrifice that could, the sacrifice of Christ.

Biblical obedience is a trust-obedience, a reliance on God's strength. Trying to obey Him is not sufficient to enable us to do the things we are commanded to. When Abraham was told to sacrifice his son Isaac, did he say, "I'll try"? No. He trusted God to provide.

The Christian life involves many commands. The only way we can obey them is by trusting God for the power. Despite this, we have a tendency to want to work at them and do them in our own strength. Many people have told me,

"I don't know why I fell. I tried to live the Christian life." That is why they fell. They *tried*. They worked at it with *their* strength rather than trusting in God and relying on *His* power for their walk with Him. If I could communicate one message to Christians, it would be to *quit trying*. You will fall, because you are leaning on yourself.

Faith is not something you crank up. Faith is our response to the faithfulness of God. "Come unto me, all ye that labor and are heavy laden, and I will give you rest" (Matt. 11:28 kjv). What saves me is not my faith; what saves me is Jesus Christ.

Trusting and trying are opposites. The Christian life is by trusting only. Jesus Christ provides the power—for your forgiveness, for your obedience, and for your everlasting life. You may believe this, or you may say, "No way." If you do not believe that Christ has given you the power for obedience through trusting Him, go ahead and keep on trying. But you will be defeated. Moreover, if you try to obey God on your own steam, you are deliberately disobeying. If you are not a Christian, and you are trying to be good because you think salvation should be for those who are good, I can at least understand that. But if you have received Jesus Christ by faith, there is no reason to live any other way than by trusting the One who has provided everything for you.

Sometimes people make resolutions and work hard at them, and nothing happens—because it is not from faith. They are trying to psych themselves into results. They want what they have seen in other people, so they try to make it come about by praying hard. They put their heads and their hands into it, but not their hearts, not their *trust*.

Faith is like sitting down. When I come into a room and I'm tired and want to rest, I get a chair. Of course, the first thing I do is I check all the legs to see if it will hold me. After that, I hook a rope to the ceiling, hang onto the rope, lower myself down, keep my legs braced, and say, "Boy, this is a great rest." Right?

No! That's silly! When I sit down, I *trust* the chair. If I sit down on an imaginary chair, I will fall on the floor. But Jesus is trustable. When you trust the Lord Jesus Christ, you quit hanging on. You don't come to the Lord by praying hard, all tensed up. You need Him, you want Him, you are ready, and the decision you need to make is to quit working at it and start trusting Jesus.

HIS ENERGY

*But now he has reconciled you by Christ's physical
body through death to present you holy in his sight,
without blemish and free from accusation. (Col. 1:22)*

Paul's ministry had an ambitious goal. What was it?
"We proclaim him, admonishing and teaching everyone with all wisdom so that we may present everyone perfect in Christ. To this end I labor, struggling with all his
energy, which so powerfully works in me" (Col. 1:28–29).
Paul's goal was to present everyone perfect in Christ. That
is a big load. How does he handle it? "Struggling with all
his energy, which so powerfully works within me." Paul
labors and struggles—with *God's* energy.

There are many missionaries and church workers out there laboring and struggling. Whose energy do some of them use? Their own. And what happens to them? Burnout. What that means is sin. We're struggling for Christ with our power. We're going to help the Lord out. We work so hard for Him that we wind up on the edge of a nervous breakdown, and we call working that way a virtue—as if God needed the help. Paul had a much bigger load than we do, but he did not get burnt out, because he did not carry the load with his own strength.

We each have a physical life and a spiritual life. God created us, and at the new birth He recreated us spiritually. He did not recreate us physically at that time. Romans 8 says that we groan, waiting for the redemption of our bodies. When the Lord Jesus Christ comes again, we will be completely redeemed, but right now, we are redeemed spirits in unredeemed bodies, bodies still subject to decay.

Our bodies are internal combustion engines. Our engines have combustion chambers which oxidize the fuel. They also have a pump, a heating system, a cooling system, and an emissions system. There are only four things we need to do to keep these engines running for seventy or eighty years: give them *fuel*, give them *oxygen*, make them *work*, and let them *rest*. If they do not get fuel or oxygen, they die. If they do not work, they atrophy. If they do not rest, they eventually go to sleep anyway.

The Bible speaks about our internal combustion engine. God said, "If a man will not work, he shall not eat" (2 Thess.

3:10b). If he is not earning his keep, cut off his fuel supply. God intends for us to use our bodies to work.

We spend most of our lives working with these engines. I make decisions, and I use my engine to work based on those decisions. If I need to shovel the sidewalk, I decide to shovel, and I take my internal combustion engine out and shovel the walk. We can use our engines to clean the garage, tidy the basement, and wash the dishes. But then the Bible says, "Present everyone perfect in Christ" (Col. 1:28). We cannot do that with the engine. "Pray continually" (1 Thess. 5:17). We cannot do that with the engine. "Love your enemies" (Matt. 5:44). Do I love my enemies the same way I shovel the snow? The answer should be obvious. That requires a different system. People try to do it with their engines anyway, and they wind up exhausted.

If the Bible tells me to pray without ceasing, I need to use what Paul used. "To this end I labor, struggling with all his energy which so powerfully works in me." That is the energy that does not end.

What is God's system of spiritual energy? When I was sixteen I worked in the Omaha stockyards. One of my jobs was stacking 90-pound bales of prairie hay. Stacking hay all day can get to be a drag. You get very dirty, very tired, and the bales are endless. Suppose I am stacking alfalfa hay, and I can see that the alfalfa is growing faster in the next field than I can stack it in this one. By the time I get this lot done, that one's going to be ready. I think, "There must be a way to do this without getting so tired." So I think and think, and I come up with a brilliant idea. It's called an intravenous tube. I put one end in my arm and the other end in my friend's arm. He sits there eating cheese while I work. I buck bales, and he gets tired.

Paul had an IV line from his arm to God. He labored and struggled, and God got tired—except that God does not get tired! Paul was refreshed because he was not using his own energy. We need to stay fresh and rejoicing, and the way to do that is to obey with God's energy, not the cornflakes we ate this morning. It is easy to make the mistake of trying to live the Christian life on food and oxygen. But you cannot love your enemy that way; no matter how hard you try, he does not get loved, and he knows it.

When it comes to doing spiritual things like praying or witnessing, I may need to use my body (e.g., when I am talking), but it is still a spiritual event. If I am trusting God in faith, I can do what I need to do and not come home exhausted. I remember one time I gave my schedule in my monthly newsletter and asked for prayer. I found out later that people had put the schedule on their refrigerator doors and prayed for me. I came back rejuvenated. I use that kind of rejuvenation as a personal sign that I am doing things God's way. I consider it sin to do what God wants but to do it my own way, without His energy.

How do you appropriate this truth? Be conscious of it before God. Say to Him, "God, I can go into this thinking I know what I'm doing because I have done this before. But I do not dare go into it unprepared." Many times I have thought something would be easy, and I could do it in my own strength. These times do not usually turn out well. *Look to God* in everything you do. Do not depend on yourself simply because you think you know what to say and what to do in a given situation.

So what is the IV line? It is continuous communication with God. It means meditation, it means time in the Word, it means prayer, it means much regular interaction between you and God. It is *an attitude of communion with Him.* But take care—you can easily make work out of the IV line, too.

My wife and I have a friend who basically lived in our house for seven years while she was getting a PhD in Classics. She did not stay overnight, but she was there from eight in the morning until eleven at night, except when she was in class teaching. She was a very disciplined woman. She would get up at five a.m., run a mile, do eighty sit-ups, and have her quiet time.

One day, I said to her, "I want you to knock off your quiet time."

She said, "Knock off my quiet time? How am I going to survive as a Christian? I have to have my quiet time or I can't make it."

I said, "You're not doing very well with it." Her time in the Book was not time with the Lord; it was work. It was something she *had to do.* She took what could have been an IV line and made it into a treadmill. I told her, "When you *want* to spend time with God and get the power, then you can come back to your quiet time." There was a wonderful change in her when she did this.

Some people are "doers." They do not know how to quit trying. Some just do not want to trust or do not know how. Their confidence is in themselves; they do Christian things with *their* power. Then they get tired, mentally and spiritually exhausted.

How can we connect the IV line with God? Well, God has already extended it to us. He reached out when He came to earth, died on the cross, and rose from the dead. The line gets attached when we receive Christ by faith, trusting in what He did for us.

Scripture describes this receiving several ways. One is the word "come." "Come unto me, all ye that labor and are heavy laden, and I will give you rest" (Matt. 11:28 KJV). Come to Him. The result is rest. Here is another one: "Everyone who calls on the name of the Lord will be saved" (Rom. 10:13). Another: "For God so loved the world, that he gave his only begotten Son, that whoever believes in him shall not perish but have eternal life" (John 3:16 NKJV). Come, call, believe: but the object is always Him. I believe in Him, I call upon Him, I come to Him. This is not a prayer of merit, but of thanks. Trust Him. Trust Him for forgiveness of sins and everlasting power for obedience.

If you have received Christ, the line is connected. *Continue to trust* the way you started. You cannot do that if you have unconfessed sin in your life. *Sin clogs the line.* Confess and repent of all the sins you have committed since you received Christ. That will open it up again.

God is reaching out to us all the time. Our problem is not how to connect the line, but why we do not *use* it. Our problem is choosing to do things our way instead of God's way. That is why many religious people are not saved; they want to be holy on their own.

God's commands are to be obeyed, and we obey by an act of the will. This act of the will, however, is not willpower. It is just a decision. When I use my internal combustion engine, I use both willpower *and* physical energy; when I carry out spiritual truths, I only use will-decision.

Let me illustrate. Suppose it is dark inside, and we want some light. We fabricate a generator out of the table and chairs—in the dark. (We are really capable.) We have nothing to turn the generator with; we could make an engine, but we cannot create fuel for it. So we hook one end of the generator up to a light bulb, and I crank the generator by hand. There is light, and we are all very pleased with it—until I get tired. Then the light begins to dim. So we put someone else on the crank, and it brightens up a little. We take turns cranking and cranking and cranking, until a little kid comes in the room and says, "What are you guys doing? Why don't you turn on the lights?" and flips the light switch. All the power of Grand Coulee Dam is behind that switch. *That* is obedience. Cranking is not.

Obedience is that simple. It just takes a decision. *Choose* to obey God. Trying is cranking the generator; choosing is flipping the light switch. The first runs on your power, and the second on the power of the Grand Coulee Dam. A lot of people are cranking away at their generators, trying to live the Christian life. They get a little bit of light, but it is far better to get the real light.

Choose to obey God. What do you do after you make the choice? Nothing. God wants us to make the decision to agree with Him, but He provides the power. "If I do not do anything, nothing will happen!" That is just what you *think*. Say, "Yes God, I will obey you," and then immediately afterwards say, "And I refuse to use my energy, so please provide the juice." "To this end I labor, struggling with all His energy which so powerfully works in me." Choose to obey Him, ask Him for the power to do it, and trust that He will give you that power.

But how do I have a quiet time without effort? I need to actually go open the Bible and read it. I cannot just sit there and get it by osmosis. I have to *do* something. How do I utilize the IV line for things that take some effort?

Let me explain with another example. Suppose you are to love your neighbor, and he is not very lovable. Do you have to *do* something? Yes. If I want to love my neighbor, and I know he does not have time to clip his hedge, I'll go clip his hedge for him. I use my body to do something kind for the neighbor.

One friend of mine, when he prayed, would tense up, clench his hands tight, and really get into it. I suspect that his prayers did not get past the ceiling, because he was *trying* to get to God. He was really going after being Christian. It is not that you do not use your physical body—it is how you use it. Paul used his body when he proclaimed Christ and admonished and taught, and I used my body when writing this book, but it did not exhaust Paul, and it is not going to exhaust me either. I am going to be fresh when I finish. But I could use the same body to do something spiritual and do it wrong. It usually takes the body to do Christian work, but many people leave out the spiritual and try to do it entirely physically, thinking that the harder they try, the more spiritual they are. Use your body—but pay attention to whether you are doing it with effort or whether you are receiving grace for it. Do not mix the two up.

There are two decisions to make: 1) Choose to obey God by His grace and 2) Refuse to start working hard at it with your own effort. "But," you say, "God says to love our children, and one of them is not very lovely. That's going to take a lot of work." The work must be based on God's energy; if you base your love on the loveliness of your child, you are in trouble, and he is, too.

Many years ago when all our children were small, my wife Bessie had intestinal flu and could not get up with the kids. We were also taking care of a 17-year-old boy during his last year of high school. About two o'clock in the morning, I heard a noise. Bessie was too sick to get up, so I jumped out of bed and went to the hallway. Off the hallway there were three bedrooms and a bathroom in the middle. I got to the doorway and stepped out. Douglas was coming from his bedroom, Heather was coming from hers, the 17-year-old boy from his, and none of them made it to the bathroom—they all vomited in the same place at the same time. And where's Bessie? Bessie's sick.

Now where do I get my love? Natural affection has just disappeared. I need supernatural love, and I *choose* it. God has already provided it, and when I choose to agree with Him, He gives me the grace to clean up the mess with joy and peace. My wife spent the majority of her life doing that sort of thing—with grace, but she chose to obey.

How do you disconnect choice from willpower? Say, "Yes, I will obey. No, I won't do it with my own energy." If

you need to bake a pie for the neighbor, the baking is sub-
sidiary to the *first choice* to love that neighbor. Keep them
separate. If you connect them all the time, soon you will
not be using God's energy. You will be running on your
own steam; you will collapse. Then you might think the
only alternative is to quit serving God.

Periodically I make trips to do evangelism and speak at
conferences and Bible studies. When I am the speaker at
a weekend conference or a Sunday service, people do not
expect me to observe a Sabbath. "Did you come down here
to do nothing?" they would say. Suppose I make a trip to
the East Coast. I speak for seven days at White Sulphur
Springs, perform a wedding on the next day, then fly to
Raleigh, pick up a car, and make a four-day trip of personal
evangelism through North and South Carolina to reach the
non-Christian parents of missionaries I know. Then I hold
an evening evangelistic Bible study with a group of Epis-
copalians, return to Raleigh, fly to Baltimore, and go back
to White Sulphur Springs for a weekend conference with
midshipmen. I do not see a single day of rest in those three
weeks. If I come home having used my own energy all that
time, I will want to die. However, I'll be coming home three
weeks behind in my work to a wife and children who want
a husband and a father, not a corpse.

When I return from that trip, I am going to return ready
to hit the road, because I will not use my own energy.

Although I use examples from my life, I have not always
done things right. In fact, the reason I know what is wrong
in this case is that I have done it wrong. I have worked

sometimes with my energy and sometimes with God's energy. I come home the first time worthless and the second time ready to go.

God turns out the lights for eight hours every day so we can sleep. He also gave us the Sabbath day for rest. Sleep is involuntary: it will happen at some point, whether we like it or not. But we try to make the Sabbath optional. The Lord Jesus said He would do God's will on the Sabbath—He would make people whole. So it is possible to work then, but do not violate the principle of rest. God gives us a Sabbath so that we can have energy for the week's work. It is a good gift. Jesus said, "The Sabbath was made for man, not man for the Sabbath" (Mark 2:27).

My Sabbath is generally Friday, not Sunday, because I am a pastor and preach on Sundays. I do not try to violate the Sabbath: but if I need to violate it for some reason, am I going to suffer the consequences of not resting, or am I going to use God's energy?

There is work you should do just to earn your keep. God expects you to get tired from that; again, that is why He turns off the lights every night. However, it is possible to work for a workaholic who does not let up on himself or you and still not get worn out. When I was on active duty in the Navy, we had a one-in-three watch. That meant that out of every 24 hours, we had 8 hours on watch. But that was not our work—our work was another 8 hours. So we had 16 hours of work, and we ate and slept in the other 8. It was not necessarily 8 hours together, either. For three years, I always had a night watch, from 8 p.m. to 12 a.m.,

12 to 4 a.m., or 4 to 8 a.m. I either went to bed at midnight, got up at midnight, or got up at four in the morning. Even with that kind of physical work, you can depend on God for extra energy.

If a man is hungry or tired, there is a chemical change in him that makes him more likely to sin. Women have similar changes once a month. It is the same when you do not have enough sleep. If you are up all night with the children, that is not spiritual work, but you will be on a short tether the next day, so pray for preventative grace. God's grace is not just there to pick up the pieces after you've shattered everybody. His grace is available beforehand, to keep you from sinning.

Once when I was running a textbook store at a college, I found myself working the ten days before fall registration when all the students come to buy their books. You can imagine what that was like. As soon as registration was over, I took a ten-day vacation to speak for InterVarsity at Cedar Campus in Michigan. That meant going from ten days of nonstop working to ten days of teaching. On the last day of teaching, I got sick. I was on my way home. Halfway there, I realized that my wife and children would be waiting for me, and I began to pray for grace so that I could come home and be a husband and a father. I called Bessie from Lansing, Michigan, and told her what time the bus would get into Ann Arbor where we lived. She said, "Wonderful; I've farmed out the kids, and I've made reservations at Leo Ping's for Chinese dinner." I got home and went out for Chinese dinner. Bessie never even knew I was sick, and I did not fake it. God gives preventative grace.

Several decades ago, Paul Tournier wrote a booklet called *Fatigue in Modern Society* (now out of print). In it, he says that you can get *spiritual* strength for a *physical* problem. It is sort of like adrenaline, but it is not adrenaline. Suppose you have to be up all night. What Tournier suggests is that you have a good time with the Lord in prayer and in the Word, and you will get physical strength for the day.

If I am very tired and have a Bible study to go to, do I go, or don't I? Normally I choose to go, and when I come home, I am physically *and* spiritually refreshed. The Word of God and the prayer and the fellowship lift me up. (This is assuming it is a good group. I have been to places where I just got worse.) You can get grace for spiritual work *and* for physical work. My suggestion is that if you are out working in the secular world, follow the same principle as if you were loving your neighbor or your enemy. If you do, people will see the difference between you and everyone else. You will be different by grace—preventative grace.

If you have a hard day, and all you want to do is complain, start thanking God. When you thank Him for everything, it is pretty hard to complain. "In everything give thanks, for this is the will of God and Christ Jesus concerning you" (1 Thess. 5:18 NKJV). If you are not thankful, confess the ingratitude and start thanking God.

If you have had a horrible day, and you are waiting for your husband to get home so you can unload on him about the kids and him and the house, because everything is falling apart, start thanking God. Thank Him for a husband and kids and everything else you are having trouble with.

"Then I won't get to complain." That is right—but you will be happier, and your husband and children will be happier. You can tell people what is wrong without complaining about it. Resist the temptation to complain.

"Therefore my beloved, as you have always obeyed, so now, not only as in my presence but much more in my absence, work out your own salvation with fear and trembling, for it is God who works in you, both to will and to work for his good pleasure" (Phil. 2:12–13 RSV). If there is anything in the Bible that sounds paradoxical, this is it. Paul tells you to work out your own salvation, and then he says God is at work in you. Here is the same passage from the New Testament in Modern English: "So then, my dearest friends, as you have always followed my advice, and that not only when I was present to give it, so now that I am far away, be keener than ever to work out the salvation that God has given you *with a proper sense of awe and responsibility. For it is God* who is at work within you, *giving you the will and the power* to achieve his purpose" (PHILLIPS).

What makes the difference between obedience to God, God's way, and obedience to God, man's way? *Willing and doing.* God gives both the will and the power. There is no mention of *our* will or *our* power.

> You have heard that it was said "You shall love your neighbor and hate your enemy." But I say to you, love your enemies and pray for those who persecute you so that you may be sons of your Father who is in heaven, for he makes his sun rise on the evil and on the good, and sends rain on the just and on the

> unjust. For if you love those who love you, what re-
> ward have you? Do not even the tax collectors do
> the same? And if you salute only your brother, what
> more are you doing than others? Do not even Gen-
> tiles do the same? You, therefore, must be perfect, as
> your heavenly Father is perfect. (Matt. 5:43–48 RSV)

Who is Jesus talking about here? Tax collectors and
Gentiles. Extortionists and pagans. Nobody could be far-
ther away from Him than they are. Jesus says if we only
love those who love us, we are no different from them.
You are doing nothing peculiarly Christian when you
love those who are lovely, when you greet those who are
friendly with you. It is natural to respond to love. Loving those who love us and greeting those who greet us is
good. But it is not Christianity.

What is Christian? Loving your enemies. How? God is at
work in us both to will and to do for His good pleasure. He
wills us to love our enemies.

You say, "All right, He wills it, so I'm going to love my
enemy if it kills me." That is choosing God's command but
trying to obey it in your strength. It is what humanists do.
They try to love the unlovely because they know it is a good
thing to do, but when they get ripped off time and time
again, they run out of love. Unfortunately, Christians have
copied the humanists, and they run out of love, too.

The difference is in the will. There is such a thing as
will-choice, and there is such a thing as willpower. English
vocabulary assumes that these are the same: for example,
when we say a "strong-willed person," we mean one who

is strong in his decisions *and* strong in his ability to carry them out. We do not make the distinction between the will to *decide* and the strength to *do*.

God does make that distinction. To carry out the impossible-sounding commands like "love your enemies," we *will* (that is, choose) to agree with God that that is the right thing to do—then abdicate our ability. Say, "I will agree with You, and God, You do it in me." It is important to make this distinction. Without it, commands like "pray without ceasing" would be nothing more than foolish idealism. Is God up in heaven laughing at all the Christians who are trying to pray without ceasing and falling asleep instead? Of course not. He very clearly means for us to do it, but *He* does it through us.

If you do not have any actual enemies, think of someone you do not like, whether it be because of his characteristics, his manner, or his attitude. Perhaps when you are around him, you get all upset and out of fellowship, so you stay away from him.

Single this person out and say, "The Lord tells me to love him, but I don't." People try to sidestep this by saying, "I love him; I just don't like him." That means they do not love him either, because they are saying that their love depends on whether he is lovable. *But that is what the pagans and the tax collectors do.* Whoever he is, whether he is your neighbor, your enemy, or your brother, you are commanded to love him, for there is no one else in the world besides enemies, neighbors, and brothers. Instead of ignoring the command, say, "I am commanded to love him. I don't love him; therefore, I am in sin. Therefore, I need to be forgiven. I'd better confess my sin." Confession involves not only the admission of sin, but an intention of *forsaking* it. It must have a sense of turning away from your bad attitude toward him, no matter how much he is responsible (in your view) for that bad attitude.

So confess it. That will not make you loving, but it will make you clean. When you are clean, then it becomes possible to love this person. However, you will not automatically love him when you confess your unlove, because loving is based on obedience, and obedience requires a will. So once you are clean, *choose* to love him with God's power.

In the Bible, the word "love" is almost always in the imperative mood. Love God. Love your neighbor. Love your wife as Christ loved the church. These are all commands. Since they are commands, love cannot be something that simply happens to you. You must *choose* to love.

Suppose you have been a liar for twenty years. You lie very quickly, very easily. You tell lies when it would be simpler to tell the truth. Suddenly you are hit with the verses that say, "God hates liars," and, "You shall not bear false witness."

You say, "Alright. I'm not going to lie anymore." What are your chances? Zero. You cannot start obeying on top of twenty years of disobedience. But if you get forgiven for those years of lies first and *then* say, "Lord, I am going to obey you and not lie," your chances of obedience will be much better. You can get forgiven and still lie again, but not as quickly or as easily.

Being forgiven makes you clean, and from a clean position you can make decisions that God will back up. He will *not* back them up if you are carrying around unconfessed sin.

So when you come across the fellow you do not love, do *not* say, "I'm going to love him." If you do, it will be phony, and he will know it. First get forgiven; then say, "God, I choose to love him," and get going. Make the choice from a clean position and start en route. It works. God takes over and gives you the love.

I have confused people on this point before. They tell me, "It seems like you are saying, 'God, I'm going to go to the park,' and then you sit down and wait for yourself to arrive there." No; there is enough in the *decision* that you make the first step to go to the park, but you trust God for the strength to get you all the way there. It is more like saying, "Lord, I'm going to go to the moon," and starting to jump. We cannot get there by jumping with our own power. We jump, and He sees to it that we land on the moon.

Christians tend to assume that they *will* to obey God, and we do not realize that we are changing the commands to fit our size. We have built-in excuses for why certain people don't get loved; we think we are obeying when we are not even close. Remember to look at the stark reality of the commandments so that when you are not obeying, you know it.

Remember that God is at work in you. Make the choice to leave yourself out of the *power* of obeying. Obey from your heart, not from your willpower. The choice to obey is yours, and the power is God's. Agree with God about what you are to do, and leave the rest to Him.

Years ago a friend told me that he was not into evangelism because the more converts he had, the more backsliders he had. That is not a legitimate reason for holding back on evangelism, but it should make us wonder why it is the case.

Here is a major reason: new Christians are not taught to live the Christian life like they were taught to receive Christ. They are taught a different way of living. How did you receive Christ Jesus as Lord? By grace. How much effort did you use? None. You *quit* trying when you received Christ. Okay: just as you received Christ Jesus as Lord, so live in Him. The Christian life should be like being born again every day.[11]

> You foolish Galatians! Who has bewitched you? Before your very eyes Jesus Christ was clearly portrayed as crucified. I would like to learn just one thing from you: Did you receive the Spirit by observing the law, or by believing what you heard? Are you so foolish? After beginning with the Spirit, *are you now trying to attain your goal by human effort?* Have you suffered so much for nothing—if it really was for nothing? Does God give you his Spirit and work miracles among you because you observe the law, or because you believe what you heard? Consider Abraham: "He believed God, and it was credited to him as righteousness." (Gal. 3:1–6)

11 A second reason so many new converts fall away is that they were not converted in the first place. The natural man cannot successfully obey spiritual commands.

Obedience means making a decision to obey God and simply trusting Him for His energy to work in us.

I would like to encourage you to pray about what you are reading here. If it is true, if it is biblical, apply it.

CHAPTER 14

"BEING" COMMANDS

*Rather he must be hospitable, one who loves what is
good, who is self-controlled, upright, holy
and disciplined. (Titus 1:8)*

O ur actions come out of what we are. *Being* holy pre-
cedes *doing* holy.

Be perfect, therefore, as your heavenly Father is perfect. (Matt. 5:48)

But just as he who called you *is* holy, so be holy in all
you *do*; for it is written: *"Be* holy, because I *am* holy."
(1 Pet. 1:15–16)

Trying to do holy things without being holy first always
turns into legalism and works righteousness.

"Finally, *be* strong in the Lord and in his mighty power" (Eph. 6:10). Being strong is not the same as exercising strength. Strength is just *there*, in the Lord.

"Let the peace of Christ rule in your hearts, since as members of one body you were called to peace. And *be thankful. Let the word of Christ dwell in you richly* as you teach and admonish one another with all wisdom, and as you sing psalms, hymns and spiritual songs with gratitude in your hearts to God" (Col. 3:15–16). These are *being* events. They precede "teach" and "admonish," which are *doing* words.

"Be kind and compassionate to one another, *forgiving* each other, just as in Christ God forgave you" (Eph. 4:32). Forgiving is a "doing" command. It is based upon *being* kind and compassionate.

"Be imitators of God, therefore, as dearly loved children and live a life of love, just as Christ loved us and gave himself up for us as a fragrant offering and sacrifice to God" (Eph. 5:1–2). God is love. That is His *being.* We are to imitate what He is just as children imitate their earthly fathers.

"Be very careful, then, how you live—not as unwise but as wise" (Eph. 5:15). Being careful in wisdom changes how we live.

> Now the overseer must be above reproach, the husband of but one wife, temperate, self-controlled, respectable, hospitable, able to teach, not given to drunkenness, not violent but gentle, not quarrelsome, not a lover of money...He must not be a recent convert, or he may become conceited and fall under the same judgment as the devil...Deacons,

> likewise, are to be men worthy of respect, sincere, not indulging in much wine, and not pursuing dishonest gain...A deacon must be the husband of but one wife and must manage his children and his household well. (1 Tim. 3:2–3, 6, 8, 12)

Most of the qualifications for elders are qualities, not actions. These qualities precede action; it is not possible to do the actions elders are to do without first *being*.

> *Be* shepherds of God's flock that is under your care, serving as overseers—not because you must, but because you are willing, as God wants you to be; *not greedy for money, but eager to serve; not lording it over those entrusted to you, but being examples to the flock*...Young men, in the same way *be submissive* to those who are older. All of you, clothe yourselves with humility toward one another, because, "God opposes the proud but gives grace to the humble"... *Be self-controlled and alert.* Your enemy the devil prowls around like a roaring lion looking for someone to devour. (1 Pet. 5:2–3, 5, 8)

This is another list of *being* commands for elders, followed by a set of *being* commands to keep the young men from being devoured by the devil.

"Wives, in the same way *be submissive* to your husbands so that, if any of them do not believe the word, they may be won over without words by the behavior of their wives... Husbands, in the same way *be considerate* as you live with your wives, and treat them with respect as the weaker partner and as heirs with you of the gracious gift of life, *so that nothing will hinder your prayers"* (1 Pet. 3:1, 7). Wives are to *be*, and husbands are to *be*. Most marriage counselors try to correct what husbands and wives *do* and *say*. That is working from the wrong end.

Notice also how the husband's *being* makes his prayers effective. Peter also addresses this:

> The end of all things is near. Therefore *be* clear-minded and self-controlled *so that you can pray.* (1 Pet. 4:7)

> For this very reason, make every effort to add to your faith goodness; and to goodness, knowledge; and to knowledge, self-control; and to self-control, perseverance; and to perseverance, godliness; and to godliness, brotherly kindness; and to brotherly kindness, love. For if you possess these *qualities* in increasing measure, they will keep you from being ineffective and unproductive in your knowledge of our Lord Jesus Christ. But if anyone does not have them, he is nearsighted and blind, and has forgotten that he has been cleansed from his past sins. Therefore, my brothers, *be* all the more eager to make your calling and election sure. For if you *do* these things, you will never fall. (2 Pet. 1:5–10)

You do not make sure of your salvation by doing the commands. Assurance comes by checking the fruit of the Spirit in your life.

> But the fruit of the Spirit is love, joy, peace, patience, kindness, goodness, faithfulness, gentleness and self-control. Against such things there is no law. Those

who belong to Christ Jesus have crucified the sinful nature with its passions and desires. (Gal. 5:22–24)

Be on your guard; *stand* firm in the faith. (1 Cor. 16:13a)

Standing is not a *doing* command like walking or running. It is *doing nothing*, like the rock of Gibraltar.

"*Be* men of courage; *be* strong. *Do* everything in love" (1 Cor. 16:13b-14). Do everything in love. This *doing* springs from the *being* which is *courage* and *strength*.

"How do I do 'be'?" The answer is, you don't.

CHAPTER 15

WILLING OBEDIENCE

Therefore, holy brothers, who share in the heavenly calling, fix your thoughts on Jesus, the apostle and high priest whom we confess. (Heb. 3:1)

L t. General William Harrison once said that the object of a Christian military officer is to get willing obedience, but obedience nonetheless. People sometimes obey when they are unwilling because of the consequences of disobedience. However, *willing* obedience is by far the best. [12]

---

12 Lt. General William K. Harrison was the chief truce negotiator for the United Nations with North Korea in 1953. Later he was stationed in Panama as Commander in Chief of the Caribbean, after which he became President of the Officers' Christian Fellowship.

"Come now, let us reason together," says the Lord.
"Though your sins are like scarlet, they shall be as
white as snow; though they are red as crimson, they
shall be like wool. *If you are willing and obedient, you
will eat the best from the land.*" (Isa. 1:18–19)

Obedience in Christ does not have to be a reluctant,
"obey God if it kills me" obedience. Because biblical obedience springs from faith and love, it can be glad-hearted,
willing obedience—and it comes with a blessing attached.

Have you ever had one boss who was kind and considerate and another who was a bear? Which did you want to
work the hardest for?

God is a loving boss. He tells the bosses on earth to use
the responsibility He has given them lovingly. He never
tells the ones on top to be "bossy bosses." He tells them to
be *kind*—husbands to their wives, fathers to their children,
masters to their slaves. That is the way God is with us. If
you have a close relationship to Him, you can be gladly
obedient because you see His commands in a different way.
They may seem impossible as words. You may still have to
say, "I don't know how to do this." That is an attitude of
humble willingness to obey, which is a far cry from fudging
the commands or refusing to obey them.

There are two ways to view God: the intellectual view
and the subjective view. The first is what we have been
taught, and the second is our gut feeling. They may be the
same, but often they are not.

I would like you to answer a couple of questions. First,
what is your gut feeling of God the Father? Do not give the

catechism answer, unless it is the same as your gut feeling. I am not asking for the correct answer from the Scripture. I want your feelings. Take a moment to think about it.

* * *

Second, what is your gut feeling of Jesus? Again, take a moment to think about it.

* * *

When I ask these questions, people generally give me views of God the Father as demanding and Jesus as loving. Although they might come up with the right answers doctrinally, many Christians are polytheists down where they live.

Once I was talking to a man who had a Christian testimony but was still in trouble all the time. When I asked him the first question, he said, "Well, if God the Father is the Creator, then He made me, and I'm a mess, so it's His fault."

"What is your gut feeling of Jesus?" I asked.

"Jesus is the one who died for our sins. He loved me enough to get me out of the trouble that the Father got me into."

"What is your gut feeling of the Holy Spirit?"

He said, "Oh, if you can plug into the Holy Spirit, you can do anything you want."

"Do you believe in the Trinity?"

He said, "Of course I believe in the Trinity."

"How do you manage to get those Three to be One?"

Where in the Bible does it say that Jesus loves me, this I know, for the Bible tells me so? Here is what John 3:16 says:

"For God so loved the world that He gave His only begotten Son, that whoever believes in Him should not perish but have everlasting life" (NKJV). Who loves us? God the Father.

I want you to read the Gospel of John and mark every reference to God the Father. Many of the references mention the Father specifically, but some just refer to God. My count in those 21 chapters is 105 mentions of the Father. Read those verses and see what they say about Him.

I am sure that if we found ourselves in the presence of God, we would be scared. But God is not a demanding boss or a corner cop waiting for you to steal an apple so He can throw you in the slammer. The Bible does not reveal Him that way. Look at John 16. This was the night before Christ was crucified:

> A woman giving birth to a child has pain because her time has come; but when her baby is born she forgets the anguish because of her joy that a child is born into the world. So with you: Now is your time of grief, but I will see you again and you will rejoice, and no one will take away your joy. In that day you will no longer ask me anything. I tell you the truth, *my Father will give you whatever you ask in my name.* Until now you have not asked for anything in my name. Ask and you will receive, and your joy will be complete. Though I have been speaking figuratively, a time is coming when I will no longer use this kind of language but will tell you plainly about my Father. In that day, you will ask in my name. I am not saying that I will ask the Father on your behalf. No, *the Father himself loves you* because you

have loved me and have believed that I came from
God. (John 16:21–27)

The Father Himself loves you. This is what we find in the
Gospel of John.

It is easy to fill your head up with correct information. If
your good view of God the Father turns out to be only your
intellectual view, put that correct information down where
you live. I may say this more than once, because it is easy
to learn truth and never put it into effect. Recognition of
God's love for you will affect the quality of your obedience
to Him. Get it into your *heart*, not just your head. The Father Himself loves you. The *Father Himself* loves *you*.

One thing that can hinder our willingness to obey is
the mistaken idea that obedience is based on our power to
carry out the commands. Our desire to obey should not be
related to our ability. Our *desire* should be related only to
God's love for us and our love for Him. Obedience is how
we express our love.

Willing obedience springs from a pre-existing desire to
obey God. If we start out by *wanting* to obey Him, He will
give us the ability. If we want to obey God, and He wants us
to obey Him, if we want to do His will, and He wants us to
do His will, there is no way we are going to miss it. There
is no way we are going to be unable to obey.

Willing obedience is ready to obey. It does not stop to
ask for a reason. Suppose I ask one of my sons to clean the
basement, and he says, "Why?" Well, there are a couple of
good answers to that one: One, it's dirty, and two, I said
so. But those are not adequate answers to a ten-year old,

because he is not asking in order to get information. He asks so that he can debate the answer, and he thinks he is the sole determiner of adequate answers. He asks because he does not want to obey.

When God tells us to do something, we do not get to say, "Why?" He does not have to tell us why, although He often does. For instance, God has given us many reasons for evangelism: the salvation of the person you are evangelizing, the condemnation of the person if he does not believe, and our reward in heaven.

> For God so loved the world that he gave his one and only Son, that whoever believes in him shall not perish but have eternal life...Whoever believes in the Son has eternal life, but whoever rejects the Son will not see life, for God's wrath remains on him. (John 3:16, 36)

> The fruit of the righteous is a tree of life, and he who wins souls is wise. (Prov. 11:30)

> Those who are wise will shine like the brightness of the heavens, and those who lead many to righteousness, like the stars for ever and ever. (Dan. 12:3)

In Matthew 5 Jesus says that if a man strikes you on the right cheek, turn to him the other also. If someone forces you to go with him one mile, go with him two. If someone sues you for your shirt, give him your other garment, too. Jesus does not tell us why we are supposed to do this. Perhaps I am in the first situation, and I cannot come up with a good reason to do it, although I could come up with what I think is a good reason to smack the other guy back. Since

I cannot come up with an "adequate" explanation, I do not obey. From studying other Scriptures, we can derive a reason for these commands[13]—but even if we never figure out why God told us to do this, are we to just disregard it? No. If we love God, we will obey Him regardless.

In the end, it all comes down to our relationship with Him: do we trust the ruler of all the earth to know what He is doing and to give us the power to do the things that seem impossible? If we trust Him for this, there will be no asking why before obeying, but rather much love, much desire, much willingness, and the obedience will happen.[14] Carnally speaking, the commands in the Bible are unrealistic. But God has given us the cross and the Holy Spirit. We have the power of obedience through Christ.

Some commands look easy, so we do them in our strength. Some look impossible, so we do not do them at all. We should always obey with God's strength through faith, whether the command seems easy or hard.

"Therefore, my dear friends, as you have always obeyed—not only in my presence, but now much more in

13 Why turn the other cheek? I believe that this is the way we are to win our enemies to Christ. Jesus came down to earth for this reason: to die for the sins of the world and to win the lost, and that is the way He went about it. That is also how He tells His followers to go about it. If we do what comes naturally—hit the guy back, refuse to go the second mile, or counter-sue him for his shirt—we will not win people to Jesus. You might think turning the other cheek will not do it either. It may or it may not, but hitting back certainly will not win him.

14 When raising our children, the rule was you could ask why, but only *after* the obedience. That provided for understanding when they genuinely wanted to know why, but it did not leave a loophole for disobedience.

my absence—continue to work out your salvation with fear and trembling, for *it is God who works in you* to will and to act according to his good purpose" (Phil. 2:12–13). We obey. God does it.

Remember the story of Gideon. He started out with 32,000 men and told everyone who was scared or did not want to fight to go home. He lost 22,000 men. He told the 10,000 who were left to go down to the brook and get a drink of water. He sent everyone home who stuck his face in the water and kept the ones who put their hands in the water and brought it up to their mouths. There were only 300 of them.

The enemy army was 135,000 strong. Gideon started out with 32,000 men, and God said, "No—too many." God told Gideon why He was doing this: if Gideon won the battle with the big army, everyone would go home bragging. But when 300 men take on 135,000 and win, there is no way they can go home and brag, because they obviously did not do it by their own strength.

When you are in a position to say, "This is hopeless; I can't do it," but you are willing, then God does it through you, and He gets the glory. This happened when Jehoshaphat went forth to fight the three enemy armies coming against Judah and Jerusalem. The Israelites prayed and said, "God, this is impossible." What was His reply?

> Then the Spirit of the LORD came upon Jahaziel the son of Zechariah, the son of Benaiah, the son of Jeiel, the son of Mattaniah, a Levite of the sons of Asaph, in the midst of the assembly. And he said, "Listen, all you of Judah and you inhabitants of Jerusalem, and you,

King Jehoshaphat! Thus says the LORD to you: 'Do not be afraid nor dismayed because of this great multitude, for the battle is not yours, but God's. Tomorrow go down against them. They will surely come up by the Ascent of Ziz, and you will find them at the end of the brook before the Wilderness of Jeruel. You will not need to fight in this battle. Position yourselves, *stand still and see the salvation of the* LORD, who is with you, O Judah and Jerusalem!' Do not fear or be dismayed; tomorrow go out against them, for the LORD is with you." (2 Chron. 20:14–17 NKJV)

Jehoshaphat trusted the Lord. He sent the choir out in front, the three enemy armies slaughtered each other, and the Israelites spent the day gathering the spoils. Do not obey with a try-obedience. Stand still and see God's salvation.

This is the kind of provision God makes for our obedience. And we settle for a mundane existence instead of an adventure. Sometimes when I was in a hard place, I had faith, and sometimes I did not; but every time I have put myself in a place to obey, God has provided the power for my obedience.

Remember, *willing* obedience is not *willpower* obedience. Put yourself in a position where there can be no temptation to obey by your own effort. Do not be foolhardy and lean over the edge of a cliff to see if you're going to fall, but do put yourself in positions that you know are the will of God, trusting Him for the ability to do what He tells you to do. Deliberately go out and stand on the promises to see if they are good. You will find out that God keeps His word.

CHAPTER 16

IMAGES OF OBEDIENCE

You also, like living stones, are being built into
a spiritual house to be a holy priesthood,
offering spiritual sacrifices acceptable to God
through Jesus Christ. (1 Pet. 2:5)

The Bible uses many parallels to teach us about the Christian life. Three of these are farming, running a long-distance race, and building. The Bible also gives two illustrations that are not pictures, but realities. They are the body of Christ (the Church) and war.

FARMING

The first parallel is farming. Please read Matthew 13:1–43, John 4:35–38, and Matthew 9:37–38. God is farming the world all the time. He wants us to participate, but the farming is always going on whether we join in or not. Obedience is required, but God gives the results.

"Then he said to his disciples, 'The harvest is plentiful but the workers are few. Ask the Lord of the harvest, therefore, to send out workers into his harvest field'" (Matt. 9:37–38). Obedience is 1) praying and 2) reaping, if sent.

"Do you not say, 'Four months more and then the harvest'? I tell you, open your eyes and look at the fields! They are ripe for harvest. Even now the reaper draws his wages, even now he harvests the crop for eternal life, so that the sower and the reaper may be glad together. Thus the saying 'One sows and another reaps' is true. I sent you to reap what you have not worked for. Others have done the hard work, and you have reaped the benefits of their labor" (John 4:35–38). Obedience is gathering the ripe harvest for eternal life.

"I planted the seed, Apollos watered it, but God made it grow. So neither he who plants nor he who waters is anything, but only God, who makes things grow. The man who plants and the man who waters have one purpose, and each will be rewarded according to his own labor. For we are God's fellow workers; you are God's field, God's building" (1 Cor. 3:6–9). Paul obeyed by planting. Apollos obeyed by watering. They both had the same purpose: increasing the harvest.

THE RACE

Athletes are taught how to win, in attitude, in strength, and in skill, always with an eye on the goal. The runner does not look at the crowd, and he does not look at the runner behind him. He keeps his eyes on the finish line and the pace-setter in front of him. Here are a few Scriptures that describe where your eyes should be. There are no competitors in the Christian race.

> Therefore, since we are surrounded by such a great cloud of witnesses, let us throw off everything that hinders and the sin that so easily entangles, and let us run with perseverance the race marked out for us. *Let us fix our eyes on Jesus, the author and perfecter of our faith*, who for the joy set before him endured the cross, scorning its shame, and sat down at the right hand of the throne of God. Consider him who endured such opposition from sinful men, so that you will not grow weary and lose heart. (Heb. 12:1–3)

Jesus kept his eye on the goal. We are to keep our eyes on Him. He is the starting gun of our race, and He is the finish line. He is our sustainer all the way. It is not a short race or a mid-distance run. It is a marathon, and it has to be run with patience.

This is the way Paul ran it:

> Not that I have already obtained all this, or have already been made perfect, but *I press on* to take hold of that for which Christ Jesus took hold of me. Brothers, I do not consider myself yet to have taken hold of it. But one thing I do: *Forgetting what is behind* and straining toward what is ahead, *I press on toward the goal to win the prize* for which God has called me heavenward in Christ Jesus. (Phil. 3:12–14)

> And we, who with unveiled faces all reflect the Lord's
> glory, are being transformed into his likeness with
> ever-increasing glory, which comes from the Lord,
> who is the Spirit. (2 Cor. 3:18)

When his race was over, Paul said, "I have fought the good fight, *I have finished the race,* I have kept the faith. Now there is in store for me the crown of righteousness, which the Lord, the righteous Judge, will award to me on that day—and not only to me, but also to all who have longed for his appearing" (2 Tim. 4:7–8).

The godly men ahead of us are our pace-setters, our examples. We are to watch them. Paul was one of those pace-setters:

> Even though you have ten thousand guardians in
> Christ, you do not have many fathers, for in Christ
> Jesus I became your father through the gospel.
> Therefore I urge you to *imitate me.* (1 Cor. 4:15–16)

> Follow my example, as I follow the example of Christ.
> (1 Cor. 11:1)

Timothy was also a pace-setter:

> For this reason I am sending to you Timothy, my
> son whom I love, who is faithful in the Lord. *He will
> remind you of my way of life* in Christ Jesus, which
> agrees with what I teach everywhere in every
> church. (1 Cor. 4:17)

> I hope in the Lord Jesus to send Timothy to you soon,
> that I also may be cheered when I receive news about

you. I have no one else like him, who takes a genuine interest in your welfare. For everyone looks out for his own interests, not those of Jesus Christ. But you know that Timothy has proved himself, because as a son with his father he has served with me in the work of the gospel. (Phil. 2:19–22)

Don't let anyone look down on you because you are young, but set *an example* for the believers *in speech, in life, in love, in faith and in purity.* Until I come, devote yourself to the public reading of Scripture, to preaching and to teaching. (1 Tim. 4:12–13)

Peter encouraged the elders to be pace-setters:

To the elders among you, I appeal as a fellow elder, a witness of Christ's sufferings and one who also will share in the glory to be revealed: Be shepherds of God's flock that is under your care, serving as overseers—not because you must, but because you are willing, as God wants you to be; not greedy for money, but eager to serve; not lording it over those entrusted to you, but being examples to the flock. And when the Chief Shepherd appears, you will receive the crown of glory that will never fade away. (1 Pet. 5:1–4)

The pace-setter is there to make us run faster and better. We are to be pace-setters for those who come behind us. As they imitate us, they should be more like the Lord Jesus. Unfortunately, not all pastors are pace-setters. They should be. "Remember your leaders, who spoke the word of God to you. Consider the outcome of their way of life and *imitate their faith*" (Heb. 13:7).

The Christian race does not have competitors, but it does have rewards.

> Those who are wise will shine like the brightness of the heavens, and those who lead many to righteousness, like the stars for ever and ever. (Dan. 12:3)

> How great is the love the Father has lavished on us, that we should be called children of God! And that is what we are! The reason the world does not know us is that it did not know him. Dear friends, now we are children of God, and what we will be has not yet been made known. But we know that when he appears, we shall be like him, for we shall see him as he is. Everyone who has this hope in him purifies himself, just as he is pure. (1 John 3:1–3)

BUILDING

All buildings require an architect, a foundation, builders, and building stones. It is the same with the church of Christ.

> "But what about you?" he asked. "Who do you say I am?" Simon Peter answered, "You are the Christ, the Son of the living God." Jesus replied, "Blessed are you, Simon son of Jonah, for this was not revealed to you by man, but by my Father in heaven. And I tell you that you are Peter, and on this rock I will build my church, and the gates of Hades will not overcome it." (Matt. 16:15–18)

Whose church is it? God's! Who is going to build it? He is!

> *For we are God's fellow workers; you are God's field, God's building.* By the grace God has given me, I laid a

foundation as an expert builder, and someone else is building on it. But each one should be careful how he builds. For no one can lay any foundation other than the one already laid, which is Jesus Christ. (1 Cor. 3:9–11)

Paul was an obedient builder.

As you come to him, the living Stone—rejected by men but chosen by God and precious to him—you also, like living stones, are being built into a spiritual house to be a holy priesthood, offering spiritual sacrifices acceptable to God through Jesus Christ. For in Scripture it says: "See, I lay a stone in Zion, a chosen and precious cornerstone, and the one who trusts in him will never be put to shame." (1 Pet. 2:4–6)

We are part of the building.

THE BODY

The church of Jesus Christ is not only a building; it is the body of Christ, made up of all believers, each with different gifts.

There are different kinds of gifts, but the same Spirit. There are different kinds of service, but the same Lord. There are different kinds of working, but the same God works all of them in all men. *Now to each one the manifestation of the Spirit is given for the common good.* (1 Cor. 12:4–7)

The body is a unit, though it is made up of many parts; and though all its parts are many, they form one body. So it is with Christ. For we were all baptized by one Spirit *into one body*—whether Jews or Greeks, slave or free—and we were all given the one

Spirit to drink. Now the body is not made up of one part but of many.

If the foot should say, "Because I am not a hand, I do not belong to the body," it would not for that reason cease to be part of the body. And if the ear should say, "Because I am not an eye, I do not belong to the body," it would not for that reason cease to be part of the body. If the whole body were an eye, where would the sense of hearing be? If the whole body were an ear, where would the sense of smell be? But in fact God has arranged the parts in the body, every one of them, just as he wanted them to be. If they were all one part, where would the body be? As it is, there are many parts, but one body.

The eye cannot say to the hand, "I don't need you!" And the head cannot say to the feet, "I don't need you!" On the contrary, those parts of the body that seem to be weaker are indispensable, and the parts that we think are less honorable we treat with special honor. And the parts that are unpresentable are treated with special modesty, while our presentable parts need no special treatment. But God has combined the members of the body and has given greater honor to the parts that lacked it, so that there should be no division in the body, but that its parts should have equal concern for each other. If one part suffers, every part suffers with it; if one part is honored, every part rejoices with it. *Now you are the body of Christ, and each one of you is a part of it.* (1 Cor. 12:12–27)

Just as each of us has one body with many members, and these members do not all have the same function, so in Christ *we who are many form one body*, and *each member belongs to all the others*. We have different gifts, according to the grace given us. If a man's gift is prophesying, let him use it in proportion to his faith. If it is serving, let him serve; if it is teaching, let him teach; if it is encouraging, let him encourage; if it is contributing to the needs of others, let him give generously; if it is leadership, let him govern diligently; if it is showing mercy, let him do it cheerfully. (Rom. 12:4–8)

Instead, speaking the truth in love, we will in all things grow up into him who is the Head, that is, Christ. From him the whole body, joined and held together by every supporting ligament, grows and *builds itself up in love, as each part does its work*. (Eph. 4:15–16)

If our body is healthy, each part of it is instantly obedient to the head and works perfectly with every other part. If the church today (made up of every Christian alive right now) appeared as a physical body, it would be spastic at best and probably partially dismembered (connected to the head but not to each other) or grossly disfigured.

If your head says, "Clap your hands," your hands should clap. If part of the body of Christ is made up of saved people represented by the right hand, whose wrist is a Reformed pastor, and by the left hand, whose wrist is a Wesleyan pastor, and the head says, "Clap," the hands would swing and miss each other by a mile. Why? Because each hand is paying more attention to its wrist than to the head.

As members of the body of Christ, we are to obey God first, not our pastors. Our *primary* obedience is to the head. This is to be instant obedience, not "I'll think about it and let you know." We must be saturated with Scripture, making our decisions in advance on biblical principles, not on the circumstances.

THE WAR

From the moment we receive Christ, we are fighting the war as part of the winning army. There is no place for receiving basic training first. Our training comes while we are under fire.

Obedience is enduring hardship, pleasing commanding officers, and not getting involved with civilian life. "Endure hardship with us like a good soldier of Christ Jesus. No one serving as a soldier gets involved in civilian affairs—he wants to please his commanding officer" (2 Tim. 2:3–4).

Obedience is fighting the good fight. "I have fought the good fight, I have finished the race, I have kept the faith" (2 Tim. 4:7).

Obedience is being strong in the Lord, wearing the full armor of God, and fighting the war in heavenly places.

> Finally, *be strong* in the Lord and in his mighty power. Put on the *full armor* of God so that you can take your stand against the devil's schemes. For our struggle is not against flesh and blood, but against the rulers, against the authorities, against the powers of this dark world and against the spiritual forces of evil in the heavenly realms. Therefore put on the

full armor of God, so that when the day of evil comes, you may be able to *stand* your ground, and after you have done everything, to stand. *Stand* firm then, with the belt of truth buckled around your waist, with the breastplate of righteousness in place, and with your feet fitted with the readiness that comes from the gospel of peace. In addition to all this, take up the shield of faith, with which you can extinguish all the flaming arrows of the evil one. Take the helmet of salvation and the sword of the Spirit, which is the word of God. And pray in the Spirit on all occasions with all kinds of prayers and requests. With this in mind, be alert and always keep on praying for all the saints. (Eph. 6:10–18)

Obedience means taking the battle to the gates of Hades and winning. "And I tell you that you are Peter, and on this rock I will build my church, and the gates of Hades will not overcome it" (Matt. 16:18). This is obedience on the offense.

Faith is unquestioning obedience with the anticipation of victory. Great faith is instant obedience. "The centurion replied, 'Lord, I do not deserve to have you come under my roof. But just say the word, and my servant will be healed. For I myself am a man under authority, with soldiers under me. I tell this one, "Go," and he goes; and that one, "Come," and he comes. I say to my servant, "Do this," and he does it.' When Jesus heard this, he was astonished and said to those following him, 'I tell you the truth, I have not found anyone in Israel with such *great faith*'" (Matt. 8:8–10).

We fight the enemy God's way.

For though we live in the world, we do not wage war as the world does. The weapons we fight with are not the weapons of the world. On the contrary, they have divine power to demolish strongholds. (2 Cor. 10:3–4)

When the perishable has been clothed with the imperishable, and the mortal with immortality, then the saying that is written will come true: "Death has been swallowed up in victory." "Where, O death, is your victory? Where, O death, is your sting?" The sting of death is sin, and the power of sin is the law. But thanks be to God! He gives us the victory through our Lord Jesus Christ. (1 Cor. 15:54–57)

But thanks be to God, who always leads us in triumphal procession in Christ and through us spreads everywhere the fragrance of the knowledge of him. (2 Cor. 2:14)

The victory comes first, and a triumph follows.

CHAPTER 17

CLOTHE YOURSELVES

*Therefore, as God's chosen people, holy and dearly
loved, clothe yourselves with compassion, kindness,
humility, gentleness, and patience. (Col. 3:12)*

In Colossians 3, Paul is speaking to born-again people,
and he gives a command. Clothe yourselves with these
things. They belong to you. Put them on as your underwear—as if they are part of you. If someone wears these
things, he will be a very soft-hearted person.

The qualities are soft, but the command which follows
seems hard: "Bear with each other and forgive whatever
grievances you may have against one another. Forgive as
the Lord forgave you" (Col. 3:13). Are those suggestions? No!

"And over all these virtues put on love, which binds them all together in perfect unity" (Col. 3:14). Love is your outer clothing. It is your suit, and all that soft, cashmere underwear of compassion, kindness, humility, gentleness, and patience is underneath. But the things underneath are what make you up because *you* put them on. You made a choice to obey God by clothing yourself in them. If you don't happen to be a compassionate person, change your underwear. It is sin if you do not.

I run into many people who had awful things happen to them when they were children. When they are aware of what happened, they become bitter and very unforgiving. I see some of the same people that professional Christian psychologists see, and in general we tell them completely different things. Here is why. *Hard teaching results in tender Christians. Soft teaching results in hard Christians.* Soft words produce Christians that do not forgive. They allow people to hang onto their bitterness longer. Hard teaching does not. We should want Christians to be soft-hearted, but we have to teach hard in order to get them to put on their soft clothes. If we take a soft approach, they will not do it.

The vast majority of counseling today is soft and prolonged. I recently had a conversation about this with some wonderful Christian counselors. They asked me, "Jim, what's your hurry?"

I said, "The Bible happens to say, 'Rejoice in the Lord always.' It also says, 'Forgive as God in Christ forgave you.'"

> Then the master called the servant in. "You wicked servant," he said, "I canceled all that debt of yours because

you begged me to. Shouldn't you have had mercy on your fellow servant just as I had on you?" In anger his master turned him over to the jailers to be tortured, until he should pay back all he owed. This is how my heavenly Father will treat each of you *unless you forgive your brother from your heart*. (Matt. 18:32–35)

Forgive when? *Now*—not six months from now. The Lord Jesus Christ saved you in an instant, and do you think He can only clean up the mess in your interior with a long, drawn-out process?

One time while giving a conference on obedience, I was talking with a woman after the last of the day's meetings. She wanted my help but did not want to tell me what the problem was. I said, "You don't have to tell me what the problem is. I don't need to know. I can tell you how to be clean tonight, or you can take the other route and dig it all out and inspect it over the next six months. The problem is this simple: it is something you did or something that was done to you. Either way, you can be free tonight.

"Now, I'm assuming the problem is something someone else did to you, because you already know what to do if it was something you did (ask for forgiveness). Here is the solution. You are feeling responsible, unclean, and guilty. You have believed the lies of the accuser. Confess to God that you have believed these lies that you are responsible, guilty, and unclean. You will be free from the sense of guilt.

"Once you are free from that, you may find out that you are bitter toward the other person. Confess your bitterness, and that will go.

"After you are free from both your false guilt and your bitterness, confront the other person. If you need help, take someone with you. But do not go guilty or unclean, and do not go with an accusatory spirit. Go to him for *his* benefit."

This works. It only fails when people refuse to take the hard teaching and put on its soft clothing. Forgiving is hard, and we do not like to do it. But if you only accept the soft teaching, you stay hard inside. When you are willing to act on the hard teachings of Scripture, you become a soft, loving Christian.

Periodically I think I may be wrong about this because everyone else seems to say the opposite, so I read one of the "soft" books. One I finished recently had some good things in it, but in the last chapter, the author said she realized she had not forgiven the other person. So she went and forgave him, which I thought was wonderful; but then she said, "Don't forgive them too soon, or you won't be able to go through all the steps." She took a list of steps with unforgiveness in her heart, then finally forgave at the end. Not only was that the way she did it: she said that is the way people *should* do it. The Bible does not say that. We are to *start* with extending the forgiveness we have received. God forgave us in Christ; that is the only basis by which we can forgive someone else, and it is unconditional. We received it unconditionally; we give it unconditionally. All her other steps were unnecessary.

CHAPTER 18

SUBSTITUTES FOR OBEDIENCE

Then the father went to the other son and said the same thing. He answered, "I will, sir," but he did not go.
(Matt. 21:30)

L et's face it: we like to obey ourselves. We like to choose what we get to do. Of course, this is not always wrong, but it is when it comes to God. We do not get to choose in our relationship with Him. Our desire should be to say, "God, I want to do what *You* choose."

One way of obeying ourselves is through works-righteousness; it is following our own rules or a set of manmade rules. Another way is volunteering. People prefer to "obey" this way because they get credit for volunteering, and they get no credit for simply doing what they are told.

Volunteering is often triggered by a challenge. Some people (called "challengers") are very good at getting volunteers. They can speak in such a way that everyone responds at the end of the speech. I believe that "challenge" is a dirty word when it comes to the Christian life. It is a manipulative appeal to the ego. Christian groups frequently use this method to get people to go to foreign missions, to memorize Scripture, to study the Bible, etc. They challenge to get Christians to do things that God has already commanded them to do anyway.

Challenges only get about a 20 percent response. When God commands, He wants 100 percent. When we challenge people to do what God has commanded them to do, fewer people obey, and they obey for the wrong motives. They act not by faith in obedience to God, but in obedience to themselves.

Quite a few years ago, I spoke on this subject at an InterVarsity conference in Virginia. After I finished my last talk, a woman came up and asked to see me right away. She said, "I'm the next speaker. I speak in twenty minutes."

"That's wonderful. I'll look forward to hearing you."

"You don't understand. I'm a Wycliffe Bible translator from Papua New Guinea, and I came here to challenge these students to go to New Guinea as Bible translators. You just ruined my whole talk, and now I've got nothing to say."

"If you are a Wycliffe Bible translator, you know a lot of Scripture. There are many wonderful things you can teach without giving a challenge."

She said, "You still don't understand. I don't know why I went to New Guinea in the first place, and I don't want to go back."

I said, "God will forgive you for going into the mission field. Confess your motives. You are trying to get other people to do the same dumb thing—go out there and volunteer rather than obey. God does not want volunteers. He wants obedient servants, and He wants 100 percent obedient servants."

Together we confessed her disobedience of going into the mission field on her own steam rather than in obedience to the call of God. She taught on something else.

The next day I was walking across the conference ground, and I saw a student with a big smile on his face. He looked very happy, so I thought I would go talk to him. I walked up and asked him what he thought of the conference.

He said, "Do you really want to know?"

I said yes.

"I think your talks have been the most boring talks I've ever heard. In fact, that last one was so bad, I was just going to pack my stuff and go home. But then that wonderful woman from New Guinea got up and spoke, and I went back to my room and became a Christian."

I was never so glad in all my life to hear that something I had said was boring. The Wycliffe translator had taught the truth of the gospel, and this young man had been converted. He would not have been if she had gone ahead with her challenge.

Challenges separate Christians: some will volunteer, and the rest will not. Everyone thinks that the volunteers mean business, that they are the godliest. In reality, they are just the fastest off the starting blocks. When I was new to Christian work, I was deceived into thinking these volunteers were obedient. They were also deceived into thinking they were obedient, and the people who didn't volunteer thought that they themselves were being disobedient for not responding to the challenge. Then I began to study the Scripture and found that Jesus did not challenge. He did not appeal to the ego. He simply commanded and expected obedience. Christians should be ready to submit their wills to the Father by faith. Almost all who volunteer do it for the difficulty and the glamour of the work. They do not volunteer for the mundane or easy tasks or for ones that are not publicized in any way. But obedience by faith means obedience in *all* areas.

Sometimes we think of Christianity like the Boy Scouts: the more we succeed in doing something, the more credit we will get. We want merit badges, so we volunteer instead of obeying.

Many years ago, I taught a junior-high Bible study that included my two oldest children. We were studying Luke 17. Jesus said to His disciples,

> If you have faith as small as a mustard seed, you can say to this mulberry tree, "Be uprooted and planted in the sea," and it will obey you. Suppose one of you had a servant plowing or looking after the sheep. Would he say to the servant when he comes in from

the field, "Come along now and sit down to eat?" Would he not rather say, "Prepare my supper, get yourself ready and wait on me while I eat and drink; after that you may eat and drink"? *Would he thank the servant because he did what he was told to do? So you also, when you have done everything you were told to do, should say, "We were unworthy servants; we have only done our duty."* (Luke 17:6b-10)

Non-trying, faith obedience does not expect a thank-you.

Well, this raised a storm in the junior-high group. They did not like it. So I asked them, "Suppose there's a dirty job in the house, and you know who's going to end up doing it. You have received revelation from God that it will be you. The job is called cleaning the basement. Now, which would you rather do: volunteer to do it, or wait until you're told? (This is assuming you cannot count on the outside chance that you won't get told to do it; it *is* going to happen.) Which would you rather do?"

None of the kids said they would wait until they were told. People only wait because they are counting on the possibility of getting out of it.

I asked the kids why they all choose volunteering, and they answered, "Because you get credit for volunteering, and you get no credit for doing what you're told."

My son Doug said, "That's not the worst of it. I'll be sitting on the floor reading the comics and thinking nice thoughts about Mom, and I decide that when I finish the comics five minutes from now I will go clean the basement for her. While I'm having all these nice thoughts of volunteering to clean the basement, Mom comes in from the kitchen and says, 'Doug, I want you to clean the basement, and I want you down there in five minutes.'"

He said, "She just ruined it all. Suddenly I don't want to clean the basement."

Why didn't he? It was the same mother he loved, the same dirty job, the same five minutes. The answer is that when you volunteer, you get to decide what you do, and you get other people's appreciation for doing it; when you are told to do something, you are just expected to obey.

One of the reasons I liked working with the military is that Christians in the armed forces are generally stronger ones. To a man in the military, obedience and authority are *good* words. Society today (Christians included) has gotten the idea that authority and obedience are bad. This is not so: when it comes to the commands of God, *volunteering* is the bad word.

Before the class was over, I asked the junior-high kids which was the greater expression of love: obeying your mother or volunteering to help her. All of the kids said that volunteering is the greatest expression of love. But it *isn't*. Did Jesus say, "If you love Me, volunteer"? No, He did not. "If you love Me, keep My commandments....He who has My commandments and keeps them, it is he that loves Me" (John 14:15, 21a NKJV). The greatest expression of love is *obedience*. Volunteering is the humanistic, works-righteousness, earn-your-way-to-heaven option. It takes faith and joy to obey.

CHAPTER 19

LEGALISM

He replied, "Isaiah was right when he prophesied
about you hypocrites; as it is written: 'These people
honor me with their lips, but their hearts are
far from me. They worship me in vain; their
teachings are but rules taught by men.'"
(Mark 7:6–7)

Many churches try to teach obedience. Unfortunately, quite a few of them are really teaching legalism. Legalism is obeying God's commands or man's extensions of them as a way to achieve righteousness. If the Church taught faith obedience, God's way, it might be accused of being legalistic, because some "Christians" are eager to stay away from obedience of any kind.

Legalism is not synonymous with hypocrisy, although some legalists are also hypocrites. A hypocrite is someone who fakes righteousness. A legalist thinks he *is* righteous. Legalists think that the form is godliness—that doing all the right things makes them godly. God will have none of it.

> Hear the word of the LORD, you rulers of Sodom; listen to the law of our God, you people of Gomorrah! "The multitude of your sacrifices—what are they to me?" says the LORD. "I have more than enough of burnt offerings, of rams and the fat of fattened animals; I have no pleasure in the blood of bulls and lambs and goats. When you come to appear before me, who has asked this of you, this trampling of my courts? Stop bringing meaningless offerings! Your incense is detestable to me. New Moons, Sabbaths and convocations—I cannot bear your evil assemblies. Your New Moon festivals and your appointed feasts my soul hates. They have become a burden to me; I am weary of bearing them." (Isa. 1:10–14)

The sacrifices and offerings mentioned in this passage were instituted by God. These people thought that simply going through the motions made them godly. Although they were getting the externals right, their hearts were far from God. What did God have to say about this?

> Shout it aloud, do not hold back. Raise your voice like a trumpet. Declare to my people their rebellion and to the house of Jacob their sins. For day after day they seek me out; they seem eager to know my ways, as if they were a nation that does what is right and has not forsaken the commands of its God. They ask

me for just decisions and seem eager for God to come near them. "Why have we fasted," they say, "and you have not seen it? Why have we humbled ourselves, and you have not noticed?" Yet on the day of your fasting, you do as you please and exploit all your workers. Your fasting ends in quarreling and strife, and in striking each other with wicked fists. You cannot fast as you do today and expect your voice to be heard on high. Is this the kind of fast I have chosen, only a day for a man to humble himself? Is it only for bowing one's head like a reed and for lying on sackcloth and ashes? Is that what you call a fast, a day acceptable to the LORD? (Isa. 58:1–5)

In the New Testament, Jesus teaches against legalists by quoting Isaiah 29:13: "These people come near to me with their mouth and honor me with their lips, but their hearts are far from me. Their worship of me is made up only of *rules taught by men.*"[15]

Paul does the same in writing to the Colossians:

Since you died with Christ to the basic principles of this world, why, as though you still belonged to it, do you submit to its rules: "Do not handle! Do not taste! Do not touch!"? These are all destined to perish with use, because they are based on human commands and teachings. Such regulations indeed have an appearance of wisdom, with their self-imposed worship, their false humility and their harsh treatment of the body, but they lack any value in restraining sensual indulgence. (Col. 2:20–23)

15   Cf. Matthew 15:9, Mark 7:7

"Touch not, taste not, handle not" is part of the *basic principles of the world* which we have died to. Legalism is not separation from the world—it is part of it.

To the Galatians Paul says, "You foolish Galatians! Who has bewitched you? Before your very eyes Jesus Christ was clearly portrayed as crucified. I would like to learn just one thing from you: Did you receive the Spirit by observing the law, or by believing what you heard? Are you so foolish? After beginning with the Spirit, *are you now trying to attain your goal by human effort?* Have you suffered so much for nothing—if it really was for nothing? Does God give you his Spirit and work miracles among you because you observe the law, or because you believe what you heard?" (Gal. 3:1–5).

And in 2 Timothy, "But mark this: There will be terrible times in the last days. People will be lovers of themselves, lovers of money, boastful, proud, abusive, disobedient to their parents, ungrateful, unholy, without love, unforgiving, slanderous, without self-control, brutal, not lovers of the good, treacherous, rash, conceited, lovers of pleasure rather than lovers of God—*having a form of godliness but denying its power.* Have nothing to do with them" (2 Tim. 3:1–5).

CHAPTER 20

TEACHING OBEDIENCE

For Ezra had prepared his heart to seek the law of
the LORD, *and to do it, and to teach in Israel*
statutes and judgments. (Ezra 7:10 KJV*)*

A ll authority in heaven and earth has been given to the
Lord Jesus Christ. *Therefore*, we must obey what He
says: *"Go and make disciples of all nations."*16

"Then Jesus came to them and said, 'All authority on
heaven and earth has been given to me. *Therefore go and
make disciples of all nations*, baptizing them in the name
of the Father and of the Son and of the Holy Spirit, and

---

16 Although mission societies tend to put a heavy emphasis on the word
"go," the sense of the Greek here is, *"As you go*, make disciples of all nations"
(cf. Matthew 10:7). In other words, *everybody* is "going" all the time.

teaching them to obey everything I have commanded you.
And surely I am with you always to the very end of the
age'" (Matt. 28:18–20). This is the key Scripture passage
on discipleship. The way to make disciples is by baptizing
them and teaching them to obey everything Christ has
commanded us.

Jesus did not say to teach all of the commands. He said
to teach people to *obey* all the commands. There are many
discipleship classes in this country, but I do not know of any
that teach people to obey everything Jesus commanded His
disciples. Christians have historically been teachers of information: we teach the commands themselves, not obedience.
We memorize the Ten Commandments and fall into the trap
of thinking that having that *information* is enough.

Over the years, many people have asked me to disciple
them. I always said no, although I knew Christians are
commanded to disciple. I refused because I knew what
those people were really saying was, "I want to be a little
Jim Wilson, and I want an inordinate amount of your time
to help me get there." I would just be making Xerox copies
of myself. I did not think that that was right, but I felt guilty
for turning people down.

Then in 1980 I went to an interdenominational conference on Vancouver Island for elders from all of western
Canada and the western United States. One of the speakers
was Vince Stryges, an elder from the Church of the Redeemer in Mesa, Arizona. During his talk, Vince said, "I
have had many people ask me to disciple them, and I have
always said, 'No.'" I sat up and paid attention. He said, "One

time I decided to say, 'Yes.' I asked the fellow who asked me to disciple him what the key passage on discipleship was.

"He came up with this one: 'Make disciples of all nations, baptizing them…and teaching them to obey everything I have commanded you.'

"I said, 'Are you a follower of Jesus?'

"The young man said, 'Yes.'

"'Have you been baptized in the name of the Father, the Son, and the Holy Spirit?'

"The young man said, 'Yes.'

"'Well, there's only one thing left for me to do—teach you to obey everything that Jesus commanded. Now everything is a lot, so you will have to cooperate. I would like you to read the four Gospels and mark every command that Jesus gave His disciples. If you have obeyed it, mark it green. If you have not obeyed it, mark it yellow. Having marked it yellow, go obey it. After you have obeyed it, mark it blue. That will turn it green. You can come to see me if there is something you do not understand. But if you understand it, just obey it. When your New Testament is green, come back and see me.'"

I thought that was wonderful, but I was too chicken to try it. Then a senior at Washington State University came to see me. "Jim, I'm in the Campus Crusade Discipleship Program. I've done it all, and there must be more. Will you teach me the 'more'?"

I said, "Yes," and I gave him the assignment I learned from Vince. "Come back and see me if you don't understand it. If you do understand it, just obey it." He never came back.

Some time later I was teaching a student at One Way Books in Pullman, Washington. After we finished, I asked him what he was doing with his life.

"I'm in the Campus Crusade Discipleship Program." I asked if anyone ever dropped out of the program, and he said, "Yes."

I said, "What do you do with the drop-outs?"

"Well, they must be back-sliding since they are quitting the program, so we give them a bad time for dropping out."

I asked if he knew the young man who had come to me for discipling. He said that he was his roommate. I asked if he was in the program.

"He used to be, but he dropped out."

"Are you giving him a bad time?"

"Oh yeah, we're giving him a bad time."

"How is he doing?"

"He's way ahead of us."

The average discipleship program is only a partial program. The eleven were told to teach their converts to obey *everything* Jesus commanded. Each of those converts was also to teach his followers to obey everything. Every Christian has to teach every convert to obey all the commands. There is no escape hatch. It makes no difference whether you are called to be an elder or an engineer. The requirement for making disciples is still there. But the major thing is to *obey everything*.

If I disobey but confess every disobedience, does that make me godly? Not necessarily. It just restores me. Imagine I come home with a large potted plant that is supposed to bloom. It is too big to set on a table, so I leave it on the floor. The next day I stumble over it, and all the dirt comes out of the pot. If I want the plant to bloom and grow, what should I do? Repot it. So I carefully repot it, only to kick it over again the next day. Out of the ensuing 365 days, I knock it over 300 days. I repot it each time. Does the plant grow? No!

The spilled dirt is disobedience, and cleaning it up and repotting is confession of sin. However, taking care of my disobedience by confession is not the same as being obedient in the first place. If I sin and confess, it makes growth *possible*, but it does not make me grow. Many Christians go through life sinning and confessing, sinning and confessing, but they never get beyond that. They do not get into *positive growth*. Is that better than sinning and not confessing? Is it better than kicking over the pot and just leaving it? Absolutely: but it is not enough if you want the plant to grow.

When I was two years old, I got scarlet fever from a cousin. We were both put in a quarantine ward in the hospital. The quarantine ward was called the pest house. In the ward, I contracted diphtheria and smallpox as well as the scarlet fever I already had. I was very ill; in fact, I did not start talking until I was three and a half years old because I was sick for so long.

Suppose you are in the hospital, and you have scarlet fever and smallpox and diphtheria and pneumonia and cancer and heart trouble. I come to see you and ask how you are doing, and you say, "Great! I don't have diphtheria anymore."

Being *less sick* is not the same as being *healthy*. Obeying everything God has commanded us is not the process of sinning less and less. Sinning less is not obedience.

We have already discussed many of the provisions that God has made for obedience: the Holy Spirit, a new nature, and not allowing us to be tempted above what we can bear, but always making a way to escape the temptation. The Lord's Prayer is also a great aid to obedience. When prayed and meant, it is the best prevention of sin, for it says, "Lead us not into temptation but deliver us from evil" (Luke 11:4). Jesus taught us to pray that. If we pray it, will He answer it? Will He not grant the request that He told us to make?

Before you get up in the morning, pray. Say, "God, it's dangerous out there. So lead me not into temptation and deliver me from the evil one." If God answers that prayer, will we be tempted less? Yes. If we are tempted less, will we sin less? Very likely.

Another means of not sinning is to store up God's Word in our hearts: "Your word I have hidden in my heart, that I might not sin against You" (Psalm 119:11 NKJV).

The Bible makes superlative statements about God's objective requirements and the provision He has given us to carry them out. The New Testament is filled with verses like this: "His divine power has given us everything we need for life and godliness" (2 Pet. 1:3).

Remember, it is not just the *information* of the commands that we need; my responsibility is to teach you to obey them. That means teaching you how to access the power to obey.

Many Christians do not even know the commands. Of those who know them, many have believed the lie of the devil that God's provision only works sometimes, for some people.

Have you ever been tempted and *not* sinned? Or do you sin every time you are tempted? How did you get past that temptation? The answer is the grace of God. By grace you did not sin. Well, do that the next time you are tempted.

God does not give grace sporadically. He provides it all the time for all the saints. Am I teaching sinless perfection? Well, *yes*. "Be perfect, therefore, as your heavenly Father is perfect" (Matt. 5:48). I do not know how our heavenly Father is perfect, but whatever He is, that is what He means us to be like. This is *not* the same as saying we cannot sin. We have already established that we can. But the Bible makes it clear that God has made it possible for us not to.

In order to teach people to obey everything, we need to get this into our heads. It is possible to not sin and possible to obey. If you do not have that mindset, you are making a self-prophesy of future sin. If you want to be obedient, consider God's requirements *and* His provision.

Let's pick a command to consider.

> Therefore I tell you, *do not worry* about your life, what you will eat or drink; or about your body, what you will wear. Is not life more important than food, and the body more important than clothes? Look at the birds of the air; they do not sow or reap or store away in barns, and yet your heavenly Father feeds

them. Are you not much more valuable than they?
Who of you by worrying can add a single hour to his
life? And why do you worry about clothes? See how
the lilies of the field grow. They do not labor or spin.
Yet I tell you that not even Solomon in all his splen-
dor was dressed like one of these. If that is how God
clothes the grass of the field, which is here today and
tomorrow is thrown into the fire, will he not much
more clothe you, O you of little faith? So *do not worry*, saying, "What shall we eat?" or "What shall we
drink?" or "What shall we wear?" *For the pagans run
after all these things, and your heavenly Father knows
that you need them. But seek first his kingdom and
his righteousness, and all these things will be given to
you as well.* Therefore do not worry about tomorrow,
for tomorrow will worry about itself. Each day has
enough trouble of its own. (Matt. 6:25–34)

God gives us several reasons not to worry. First, Jesus
says that the flowers and the birds are not worried, and God
takes care of them; and we are more important than they
are. Second, worrying is what the pagans do. Do you want
to copy the pagans? Third, your heavenly Father knows
that you need these things. He knows that He did not make
you with fur. He knows that He made you with a stomach.
He made the needs, and He will make the provision.

How are we to not worry? "Seek first His kingdom and
His righteousness, and all these things will be given to you
as well." *Do not focus on the need*—that is God's business.
Focus on His kingdom and His righteousness, and God will
take care of the need.

"Therefore do not worry about tomorrow, for tomorrow will worry about itself. Each day has enough trouble of its own." Is that true? Like Mark Twain said, "I've had many troubles in my life, most of which never happened." The way to keep from worrying is to focus on the kingdom. Keep your eyes on Jesus.

People who work in faith ministries often fall into the trap of putting their faith in faith. They are focused on not worrying. This is like trying to forget something. Trust me: it does not work.

Once I was working for a Christian ministry that was in financial trouble. We were part of a larger ministry, and the larger ministry was not very ethical. We got involved in the debt that the larger ministry incurred. Our part of the debt was about three thousand dollars.17 So I prayed and I worried and I prayed and I *worried*. We had a commitment not to raise money from people and only to pray to God for finances. So I prayed, but I was focused on the problem.

One Monday morning I was in the shower, and I suddenly knew that God had answered our prayer for the three thousand dollars. It was such an overwhelming assurance that I told my wife that God had answered our prayers, and we did not need pray for the money anymore. I told the treasurer of the corporation the same morning. I could not explain it. About noon that day I got a phone call from a stockbroker in New Jersey who said that one of his clients had told him to sell three thousand dollars worth of stock and send it to me. He was calling

17 This was in 1961. $3,000 then would be about $24,000 now.

to find out how to make out the check and what address to send it to.

This has happened quite a few times in my life. My wife would see it happen, so the next time we would get into financial trouble, she would say, "Say we've got the money. You said it last time." Of course I would want to say it, so I would put my faith in my faith—a dumb place to put it. God said to seek first the *kingdom*. Look to Him first, and He will look after everything else.

The best way to teach obedience is to be an example of obedience. The best way to learn obedience is to follow an example.

> Do not cause anyone to stumble, whether Jews, Greeks or the church of God—even as I try to please everybody in every way. For I am not seeking my own good but the good of many, so that they may be saved. Follow my example, as I follow the example of Christ. (1 Cor. 10:32–11:1)

> Therefore I urge you to imitate me. For this reason I am sending to you Timothy, my son whom I love, who is faithful in the Lord. He will remind you of my way of life in Christ Jesus, which agrees with what I teach everywhere in every church. (1 Cor. 4:16–17)

Remember that there are two ways of teaching truth. We can teach from the teacher's head to the student's head, or we can teach from the teacher's heart to the student's heart. The second is the way to teach obedience. The truth needs to get past our intellectual assent down to where we *live*. How do we teach this way? If you love God, love the command, and love the students, your words and your actions will be wrapped up in love.

EPILOGUE

Here is what I hope I have communicated about obedience:

- We are dead to sin, the flesh, the law, and the basic principles of this world. We died with Christ. We are crucified with Christ.
- We are alive in Christ, risen with Him.
- Because of the Cross, we can meet the righteous requirements of the law.
- We use God's energy to do this.
- We obey by the power of God's grace, the same way we received Christ.
- We are to look at the commands in the Bible just as they are. Are there any that are too big to obey? Not with God. Not with His grace and His strength. This is trusting: no trying allowed.

Through the Cross, God made it possible for us to live the righteous requirements of the law. We do this the same way we were saved: by trusting Him to give us the ability through His strength. Then we look the commands in the eye and say, "Yes, Lord."

It is possible for you to agree with everything you have just read and not get it past your mind. These things should speak truth to your heart as well. That is where true obedience comes from. If you agree with what you have read here, get the truth into your heart. How do you do that? *Thank God* for each truth. *Keep on thanking Him!* This is meditating.

> Blessed is the man who does not walk in the counsel of the wicked or stand in the way of sinners or sit in the seat of mockers. But his delight is in the law of the Lord, and on his law he meditates day and night. (Psalm 1:1–2)

In the Lord Jesus Christ,
JIM WILSON

EXCERPTS FROM

THE FATHER
AND HIS FAMILY

BY E.W. KENYON

THE DUAL THEORY

Many believe that when a man is born again he receives Eternal Life but that the old nature is not removed, and that these natures war with each other in the new creation.

They base this teaching upon the seventh chapter of Romans.

This is not the experience of a believer but of Paul as Jew under the Law.

This chapter is a treatise on the Law showing the relation of the Law to the awakened conscience of a Jew, who has not been recreated.

If the reader will turn to this Chapter and read it carefully, he will see that the whole argument is the argument of a Jew before he has been born again.

He says, "I was alive apart from the law once; but when the commandments came, sin revived, and I died and sin finding occasion, through the commandment beguiled me, and through it slew me."

The believer is not under the Law; he has nothing to do with it whatever.

The Law belongs only to the Jew.

Again he says, "For we know that the Law is spiritual; but I am carnal, sold under sin."

We Gentiles were never under the Jewish Law.

We know that the believer is not sold under sin: he has been made free from sin and has become a bondservant of righteousness.

Again Paul says, "For that which I do I know not: for not what I would, that do I practice; but what I hate, that I do."

This is not the experience of a child of God, "But if what I would not, that I do, I consent unto the law that it is good," (but ye are not under the Law but under grace) so now "it is no more that I do it, but sin which dwelleth in me."

Sin does not dwell in the believer.

Here sin is spoken of as something that was dwelling in Paul.

If sin has a habitation in the believer and the believer is a subject of it, then God is united to sin, or in other words, to the Devil.

"I find then, in regard to the Law, that to me who would do good, evil is present.

"For I delight in the Law of God after the inward man: but I see a different law in my members, warring against the law of my mind, and bringing me into captivity under the law of sin which is in my members."

The Ten Commandments are the Law of Sin; they are the revealer of Sin.

They told the penalty of sin, and Paul delights in the Law from an intellectual point of view but he found another law working in his mind; it was the Law of Sin and Spiritual Death.

SONS ARE FREEMEN

The believer is free from the Dominion of the Law.

The believer is free from the Dominion of Sin.

The believer is free from the Dominion of Spiritual Death.

The believer is free from the Dominion of Satan.

The believer is now under the Dominion of the Grace of God, and Jesus is his Lord.

Could a child of God utter this cry? "Wretched man that I am! who shall deliver me out of the body of this death?"

That is not the language of a child of God; that is the language of a Jew under the Law who has seen his actual condition and has also seen the possibilities of Redemption in Christ Jesus our Lord.

In Gal. 5:16–18 is another proof-text of the Dual Nature Theorist:

> But I say, Walk by the Spirit, and ye shall not fulfill the lust of the flesh.
>
> For the flesh lusteth against the Spirit, and the Spirit against the flesh; for these are contrary the one to the other, that ye may not do the things that ye would.
>
> But if ye are led by the Spirit, ye are not under the law.

CONTRAST

In this Epistle Paul is contrasting the Jew under the Law and the believer under Grace, for the Book of Galatians is a book of contrasts.

It is a contrast of Law and of Grace.

It is a contrast of Faith and Works.

It is a contrast of Sons and Servants.

It is a contrast of Circumcision and the New Birth.

It is a contrast of Promise and Law, of Flesh and Spirit, that is Natural Man and Spiritual Man.

It is a contrast of Christianity and Judaism.

It is a contrast of Love and Legality.

We know that Man is a spirit.

We know that he lives in a physical body.

We know that nearly all the sins that are committed are committed through physical senses.

We know that these physical senses can become distorted, dissipated, abnormal so that they will crave unnatural gratification.

We know that the believer's life is a battle with his physical body.

The reason for this is that we are not normal human beings. Parental sins have set our teeth on edge.

We are living in the realm of Spiritual Death where Satan is the Emperor.

Most of the people with whom we associate are under the Dominion of the Devil.

Satan's appeal always comes through the physical senses; so Man's only hope is to live in the spirit.

I don't mean the Holy Spirit, but in his own spirit realm; instead of dreaming of gratifying physical passions or desires, he is to live in the realm of the spiritual, his own spirit fellowshipping with the Spirit of God.

This is the only way to overcome the influence of his physical body upon himself. So Paul says here, "If we walk by the spirit," more literally if we walk in the realm of the spirit, "ye shall not fulfill the lust of the flesh," for the members of your body are combating against your spirit, and your spirit is contending against your flesh or the members of your body.

TEMPTATION AND SIN

The cries of your physical body are not sin, but if you yield to them it is sin. Every appeal of Satan will come on this level; so there is going to be a combat until your physical body is brought into subjection to your spirit. But if you let the Holy Spirit dominate your spirit He will lead you out into liberty and victory over these temptations. He will bring your physical body into perfect submission; so that your life will be tranquil, pure, and victorious...

DUAL NATURE DILEMMA

There is nothing wrong in the physical body, but if you turn it over to the Devil and allow him to work through it, it will destroy the spirit.

God gave us our body as a servant; we are to rule it, but if the servant rules us, it is anarchy and confusion.

If man is not a New Creation but simply receives a New Nature plus the old Nature, we are led into a strange dilemma.

We know that this old Nature is Satanic Nature, Spiritual Death; then the man who has received this New Nature has two Natures, the Nature of God and the Nature of the Devil.

He belongs to two families, the Family of God and the Family of the Devil.

Satan has a legal right to rule over his part of the Nature, and God has a legal right to rule over His part.

This gives to man a double nature. One is Doctor Jekyll, and the other is Mr. Hyde: legally a child of God, and legally a child of the Devil.

To follow this out logically, one half of man can go to Hell, and the other half, to Heaven.

The Theory would be humorous if it were not so serious; but the problem is when does man get rid of this Satanic nature.

The answer is, at Death.

We know that Death is of the Devil; this leads us into a still worse dilemma.

If this is so, the sacrifice of Jesus Christ has failed in its object.

The man who has accepted Him as his Savior is only partly saved, and he is not redeemed.

Satan still has a legal right to rule over him.

Jesus Christ is obliged to divide His Dominion with the Devil. This is humiliating.

The Fall of Man was a finished product; the Redemption is a fumble.

The New Birth is a hybrid, a bitter failure.

The humiliating part of it is that according to this theory God is obliged to seek the Devil's assistance in order to perfect Man.

Death, the first child of Satan, is to put the finishing touches on the New Creation, God's child. If Man is cleansed or made free from the Adamic Nature by Physical Death, why was it that God did not permit Physical Death to save the whole human race, for all die?

This thing is too abhorrent to even contemplate.

It makes God justify a child of the Devil or a hybrid at the best.

It makes God unite Himself with the Devil in the human.

It makes Jesus' statement, "I am the vine, ye are the branches" grotesque.

It makes Satan, our destroyer, in the end our redeemer.

The heart shrinks from this teaching.

We believe that the New Birth is a New Birth.

We believe that the New Creation is a New Creation.

We believe that God was able to do as finished a work in Man's Redemption as the Devil did in his Destruction.

We believe that the New Birth glorifies God, magnifies Jesus Christ, and exalts the human.

It is not a desirable task to array one's self against the common teachings of the Church, especially of those who are among the most devout and deeply zealous of all the Family of God, and I know that my readers recognize that I do not come to these great experimental teachings of the Church with the spirit of resentment or hostility, but as a fellow-member of the body of Christ who believes he has an answer to these problems that have agitated the Church during the last hundred years.

The writer loves the members of the Family as he loves himself and would speak with the freedom that love gives on these great themes.

The fact that in the new birth we actually receive the nature of God has not been majored by the Church. This has led us into many difficulties as we have already seen.

One very devout group talks much about Justification and Adoption.

It would seem as though the fact of the New Creation, as a New Creation, had never been given serious consideration.

They teach that when one accepts Jesus Christ as Savior that God justifies him of all that he ever did; that is, He forgives him of his sins, but He does not remove the sin nature, the cause of his sins.

This step which is called conversion is considered simply a preliminary.

The real work is known as the Second Work of Grace, or being Wholly Sanctified.

This Second Work comes to the convert only when he has surrendered himself utterly to the Lord, has repented deeply, and has sought diligently for a clean heart.

They do not believe that the heart is made clean at conversion, as that term is used.

They make a distinction between sin and sins.

Sin is what we are by nature; sins, what we do.

Many of their teachers have believed that when one is converted he receives the Holy Spirit in a limited measure, and when he becomes wholly Sanctified the Spirit fills the temple.

They also teach that one can lose this gracious blessing of a clean heart, or Sanctification, by the slightest known sin.

For this reason the majority of those who go to the altar and honestly seek for this blessing lose it in a few weeks or months after the struggle for it.

Those who are familiar with Mr. Wesley's Journal remember that he was confronted with this same difficulty when he returned in his itinerancy, that in some places many who had received this Second Work of Grace and rejoiced greatly in its reception, were found under a cloud, backslidden, and the work needed to be done again.

This teaching has produced an unstable and vacillating type of Christianity.

It has made the recipient skeptical of himself and others.

It has not been a healthful teaching, but it has produced in the face of all this, by the Grace of God, some very devout Christians.

REPENTANCE

Repentance means a turning around or a change of mind. True repentance is turning away from sin and also turning toward the One who died and rose again. The Bible calls this "repentance toward God and faith toward our Lord Jesus Christ." It is an about-face. It is not a sorrow.

> Even if I caused you sorrow by my letter, I do not regret it. Though I did regret it—I see that my letter hurt you, but only for a little while—yet now I am happy, not because you are made sorry, but because your sorrow led you to repentance" (2 Cor. 7:8–9a).

You could stop at "sorry." There is God-intended sorrow and non–God-intended sorrow.

> For you became sorrowful as God intended and so
> were not harmed in any way by us. Godly sorrow
> brings repentance that leads to salvation and leaves
> no regret, but worldly sorrow brings death. (2 Cor.
> 7: 9b–10)

If a man is sorrowful over his sin as God intended, it leads to a turn. When he makes that turn, however slight, God is there with His grace, and he is saved. It is Jesus Christ that does the saving, not the repentance. But people can run away from grace and stay sorrowful. If they go through life sorry, they will die sorry. There is no virtue in sorrow, no saving work in sorrow, no merit badge in sorrow. The sorrow of the world leads to remorse and death, but godly sorrow causes repentance and leaves no regret. Grace takes care of it. If you have regret, it only proves that your sorrow is worldly sorrow. If I sin today and am sad and sorry about it and am still sad and sorry tomorrow, that proves that I did not repent of it today.

Can you regret the grief you have caused other people? When Bessie and I were first married, I would find out I did something wrong. I would be sorrowful to repentance. I would turn to God and confess and get forgiven. I would turn to Bessie and tell her I was sorry. And she would think, "If he's sorry, how come he's so happy? How come there's no regret?" Paul says that godly sorrow does not leave regret. I was happy because I had been forgiven by God. I did not need to crawl for two weeks.

The enemy accuses you and keeps you under that bondage of regret. It is not from God. I know that it is natural to want to say, "I'm sorry, I'm sorry, I'm sorry," to the victim for the rest of our lives, but that will not help him a bit. This does not mean you should go through life glad that you crippled someone else. But if you repent, you will be cleansed and able to live a life of joyful obedience to God, which is far, far better for everyone than moping in your sin.